This is Why

This is Why

James Weber

Webalization, Ethel LA. Publisher

Published by:

Webalization LLC
Ethel, LA. 70730

10 9 8 7 6 5 4 3 2 1

First Edition © 2019 by James Weber

ISBN: 978-0-578-60043-7

Acknowledgments

When one engages in an endeavor such as this, there are always people who deserve thanks. The fear when writing a thank you note is that you will leave someone out. In this particular case, there is one person above all I would like to thank. How does one say thank you to someone who inspires you simply by being who she is? She is my motivation to be better than I was yesterday. She is the first person I see in the morning and the last person I see at night. I speak with her ten plus times throughout the day. No matter what I do, she expects it will be a success, yet, still tells me I can do better. She is the driving force for me to do better. She is the standard for my best. I know I can do better because my wife is proof of how well I can do.

Cynthia, wife, mother, guiding light or whip-bearing pursuer; you have been everything I have needed since before I knew I needed you. Thank you, and love always.

There are also my sons, James Jr. and Jordan, who have hindered my speedy completion of this endeavor by asking me a thousand questions every time I am trying to work. They are, however, the motivation to be the best father I can be. Because of them, I shall endeavor to be the best that I can be because I know that four little eyes shall always be focused on me. Thank you, gentlemen.

Getting to Know the Contents

1

What is a Police Officer?

The best definition of a police officer would be a problem solver. More to the point, he or she is a member of a paramilitary organization put in place by the local government to enforce the laws and maintain the rights and safety of the people in that jurisdiction. The officers are to be trained in a uniform way to handle an assortment of crimes and scenarios.

2

Introduction

Today, there is a vast chasm that is open and widening between the police and the people they serve. There exists, in some places, a moniker on police officers that makes them the bad guys. This, of course, is a biased view. What is the bias based on? Some would say the bias is based on individual experience. Some would reason the bias is based on culture. Some would even say the bias is based on police actions that throw a negative shadow on departments everywhere. I would say they are all correct. I would also venture the bias is based on ignorance—an ignorance of what a police officer is, what his job is, and how that job affects you.

Have you ever seen the videos on *YouTube* where a police officer is making an arrest? You listen to the video and form an opinion about the event. If you were to watch a video with the sound off, as opposed to the video with sound on, you might have a different opinion of the events.

Please do not misconstrue what I'm saying. There are injustices out there. There are officers who misbehave. It is all the more dangerous when an officer does not do his job fairly and impartially. What I am saying is that police officers are individual people who decided to do a tough job. There are racist police out there. There are sadomasochistic police out there. There are police out there with their own agendas. Unfortunately, an asshole with a badge is still an asshole. We are not here to address them today. We are speaking of the actions of the vast majority of police who signed up to be a force for order.

The purpose of this book is to give the civilian an insight into police mentality. The best way to provide you with insight is to explain some of the situations officers are faced with on a daily basis. I will attempt to give you a sample of my limited experience (bask in my modesty). I will try to convey what I was thinking and feeling in multiple situations that are common among most police officers in multiple fields. I will try to guide you without adding personal bias to situations. I'm hoping that with a look inside my train of thought, perhaps my intentions will become a little bit clearer.

I am a police detective. I have nineteen years of experience in law enforcement. I was on the streets as a uniformed patrol officer for seven years. I have been a detective for eight years. I have been a badge carrier even longer. I've been around police officers of numerous agencies. I have grown up in the neighborhoods in which I now police. I've seen the situations from both sides. I've even had my share of run-ins with the police before I joined them. I have worked nearly every kind of investigation from misdemeanor theft to espionage to homicides. I have worked an assortment of sex crimes, but I'll admit my experience is limited due to my personal feelings toward those types of crimes. While I do not have full authority on the types of crimes I work, I do have some latitude.

Please take this journey with me. Learn a few things. Get to know not just me but police officers in general. I hope we can come out on the other side of this together with a better understanding. Please understand, I'm not about to give away anything that would put any officer in danger.

3

Getting to Know the Officer Personally

As a police officer, a veteran police officer, I come into contact with an assortment of people in a great many situations. Every situation is different and must be handled as such. With so many options available, how are decisions made? I'm speaking of life or death decisions that must be made at a moment's notice. Any officer can tell you, training and experience. That is the difference between a civilian and a police officer. As police officers, we repeatedly train to respond a certain way. Regardless of what people think, we are not trained to aim for the legs. We don't give warning shots. We also rarely receive second chances. We are not taught "superhero" moves that work on everyone. There is not a secret grip that is going to turn that 6'4," 260lbs man into a 5'4" manageable problem. There is nothing out there that's going to make me 6'2." Like a lot of agencies, we rarely patrol two men to a car. Dispatch doesn't always send two units. We don't always know what's happening before we get there. And one of the biggest issues is we don't always know what you are going through. Ask any officer who has been on the job for more than a year if he's had an "oh shit" moment, and I'll bet he can tell you about two or three.

The catch twenty-two for an officer is that we must appear

to be friendly while also appearing to be invincible. We must appear to be human while doing a job that, by its very nature, requires one to be detached. How do you get the suspect's information if your eyes are full of tears? How do you convince her that she shouldn't keep taking him back while at the same time being unable to offer her any assistance in paying her bills? I'm unable to find her a new place to stay tonight or provide her the necessities that she requires and he provides. As a police officer, I know the law. I know which laws he violated when he beats her into submission. I know what to charge him with so that he can possibly face the time he deserves. However, as a police officer, like most police officers, I have no idea about the bond process. She does. She can tell you just how long he is going to be in jail. She knows when he is going to be calling. She knows how long they will hold him before he is released. She knows how much it will cost to get him out. She also knows that when he calls her and tells her to come to get him, and she doesn't, she knows who he's calling next. She knows how much the electric bill is. She knows Junior needs school uniforms by next week. She knows his mother babysits her baby while she is at work. She knows daycare rates are ridiculous. She knows all these things before she calls the police. She also knows that this hurts and she wants it to stop.

I'm no cold-hearted villain. I feel just as you do. I have all the emotions of the spectrum, but you would be surprised at what one can get used to. If I see a beautiful young lady beat to a pulp, it's a horrifying sight. When I see the same young lady beat to a pulp for the fourth time, it doesn't carry the same shock. I know how this sounds. As I write the words, I can't help but reassess them again and again. Regardless, I know them to be true. I have seen some horrible things in my time. When I see these things, I don't cry. I don't always feel empathetic. After a while, it does start to become a blur. There will always be special cases that tug at an officer's emotional heartstrings. These cases usually involve things that make the case personal. If the officer sees a child hurt, and he has a child around that age, he is liable to take that case more personally. This could be a good thing because he will leave no stone unturned. It could be a liability as well. The officer could look so hard for a bad guy that his judgment is clouded, and he makes a mistake. A mistake seems like a small thing but when someone who has committed a heinous crime goes free because of it, its huge. If the wrong person is punished, that's a mistake I can't live with. Like most officers, I would rather the bad guy goes free than get the wrong person. It is also true that if you search for something hard enough, you will find it, even if it's not there.

The next time you run across an officer, think of the things he has seen. He won't want to talk to you about them, but he has seen them, and they do not go away. This cloud becomes a part of the officer. Officers tend to be cynical because they end up seeing the world from a different angle.

However, they are human and know the importance of laughing. Officers are some of the best jokers you will ever meet. If you are able to observe them at the district, you will see they play, joke and laugh constantly. You can liken them to a group of high school kids (without all of the romantic drama). Unfortunately, they are some of the biggest practical jokers as well. Jokes can get out of hand pretty quickly. Beware, rookies.

This twisted sense of humor is what has gotten a lot of officers in hot water. We are supposed to remain professional at all times. That's kind of like flexing a muscle. It's easy at first, but the longer you hold it, the harder it gets. When you see a bunch of officers at a scene, and they have been there for two hours, you will see they relax. They start joking with each other. They start laughing and horsing around. The fact that there is a body on the ground at the center of the laughter is the problem.

To laugh when you should cry is not unheard of. Pseudobulbar affect is when someone laughs at inappropriate times. I wouldn't go so far as to say officers suffer from pseudobulbar affect, but they most certainly have a different outlook on things. I have found myself making jokes that in any other company would be deemed entirely inappropriate. However, with my coworkers, I have found that they get it and are just as bad. I have wondered if the job attracts people who have this twisted sense of humor or creates them. I would assume the latter.

When I started the police academy, I had no family. When I say family, I mean a wife or children. My life was my own. If I lost it, it would be sad, I'm sure, but the repercussions wouldn't go too far beyond myself. Once I got married and promised that I would share my life with someone else, that changed. Once I had a child, it changed even more. I began to think differently. I became more cautious. I would search a guy that second or third time even though I watched the rookie search him just moment's prior. I would even go so far as to say that I became...afraid.

The Royal Marines have a saying, "Fear is not to be feared. Fear is to be respected." Fear can be both the best and worst motivator available. If fear causes you to act out of character, it's a bad thing. If it motivates you to excel for fear of failure, then it is an ally. No matter how hard you strive, you will make mistakes. The practice and constant attention to detail will make those mistakes smaller and less consequential.

If I had to critique the biggest mistake a rookie officer makes, it would be not to listen to his training. The second biggest mistake would be to listen to his training. I'm aware that this statement is contradictory, but so is police work. We are supposed to be a part of a populous but also outside of it. We are supposed to be the authority but not be in charge. In the academy, they try to teach you to take command of the scene. In the real world, some people won't be led.

How can you, as a police officer, go into a man's house and start giving orders? You are in his castle. It's a tough situation. When you tell the king of that castle to calm down and have a seat, will he listen, or will he say, "This is my house"? I know what I would say. I also know that the answer could switch your problem from one scenario to the next in the blink of an eye.

If you can recall back when you were a young lad among your friends, there was a leader. In every group, there's a leader. One person would say, "Hey, let's go to the mall," and each person would decide whether or not they were going to the mall. The leader, however, would say I'm going to the mall, and everyone else would simply go. This is a trait of a leader. He is not quite leading by example, more so taking his own path and others want to follow. It's just as simple as that. A person like that is both admirable and unpredictable. This is a trait and not really something that is easily taught.

When I tell the "king" of the residence to have a seat and calm down, I mean it. The inflection in my voice says I mean it. The polish of my boots says I mean it. The fact that my uniform is pressed and all of the leather gear is well maintained says I mean it. While I was in the academy, my sergeant used to emphasize "omnipresence." It's a way to make a statement without opening your mouth. It's the ambiance you create and bring with you. It could easily save your life. People judge us by our appearance. It's not fair, I concede. But to ignore it simply because it's not fair is beyond naïve. It's stupid.

Coming back to my initial statement, I say the biggest mistake is both listening to your training and not listening. By all means, listen to your training. Also, understand that your training is not infallible. Your training is meant to guide you in your actions. It is impossible to predict all of the situations you, as a police officer, will encounter. So, don't get stuck in a single course of action because of your training.

A good police officer will look the part. That's not to say the officer with the huge belly or baggy clothes has nothing to offer. Often, these are the supervisors, and they contribute experience. But, and I emphasize this, if you are on the street working, you should look the part. In my experience as a man (been one my whole life), I know we size each other up. As soon as a man walks into the room, we check him out. It's kind of like, "Am I still the alpha male here? Yeah, it's me. I'm the man. He's got nothing on me." It's a minor thing that a lot of men do. When a police officer comes into a room, people do the same thing. If his uniform is dirty, you think less of him. Most people would think less of any professional with a dirty uniform. For an officer, it could mean that person who he is about to arrest thinks, "I can take this guy." It may be as simple as, "You can't even iron your uniform. How can you presume to give me orders?" The situation will still get resolved, but it may be just that much harder. I know you may think that this line of thinking is a stretch, but take a minute to think about it. Have you ever watched an athletic competition, perhaps a UFC fight where one of the guys is ripped to the shreds? He has a six-pack and huge arms that show every muscle possible. Perhaps the other guy is a bit chubby. Perhaps he is unshaven with a little gray in his beard. While everyone loves an underdog, who would you place your bet on? The underdog is the underdog because he is not expected to win. It doesn't matter who is actually the better fighter. You will likely place your money on what you would deem "the safe bet." Perhaps you would take your chances for the big payout. If we were playing for higher stakes like say, your life, I'm sure the safe bet would be your bet. It's a small advantage but one worth having.

Officers, as a rule, are paranoid. At least that's what the civilian would call it. I call it being hypervigilant. We need to be constantly aware of our surroundings. If we are in a business, we want to be the first to know who enters. We would like to know who is in the residence when we enter. You are rarely going to see one officer eating a meal in a restaurant. If you do see a single officer, he is going to be at the back of the restaurant away from the door. He is going to be positioned so he can see everyone who enters or leaves. The officer is actually just trying to enjoy his meal. He also wants to give himself the maximum amount of time to react to a situation. Even off duty, a police officer tends to be the same way. A police officer's spouse has to make adjustments for the officer. She has to wait for a seat in the back of the restaurant to be available. She has to allow him to sit in a position that allows him to see the door. Like I said, this does appear to be paranoia, but let's be honest, if a bad guy walks in, who is getting shot first?

With that being said, let's try to understand when you approach an officer while he is eating, and he appears annoyed. He doesn't know if you are coming to shake his hand or harass him for arresting your cousin. I absolutely do not want to discourage anyone from being social with the police. That is not my intention. As I have said, I am trying to help you understand. While we are on this topic, let me speak on another thing that officers tend to be too polite to point out. Stop telling your children the police are going to get them. Don't give your kid the impression that we are the bad guys, and we are going to punish them for frivolous things. We will not, and I will not participate in your shenanigans. Furthermore, I want the kid to look at police and see someone who can and will help them when they need it.

4

Police Lingo

I would like to go over a few phrases that I am certain will come up often in any productive conversation with a police officer. Most organizations, fraternities, clubs or groups develop their own phrases that have no meaning beyond that group; police are no exception. Police have their own jargon and language that can be understood immediately by other officers to convey a complicated idea quickly and concisely. I won't be able to mention all the different words and phrases police use. I can give you some of the most common. They will be different from department to department. These are some that I have come to see are universal as opposed to just my department.

"Oh Shit" Moment

I have previously mentioned an "oh shit" moment. An "oh shit" moment is a situation that, in most cases, stems from a misjudgment by the officer. When I say misjudgment, I mean, the officer thought this was a case of children left at home by themselves only to find out these kids are being held at gunpoint by their estranged father. The "oh shit" of this situation is the officer approached the situation in a calm, nonconfrontational manner to keep from scaring the children. He walks across the yard, and he knocks on the door, only to find out there is someone dangerous inside. This relaxed demeanor puts both the officer and the hostages at risk. He must immediately transform himself from that friendly officer into a tactical specialist. This is always a possibility, and that is why we are taught to stay vigilant at all times. When we forget this lesson, it is often retaught in the field with absolute clarification. The bottom line is, the "oh shit" moment is an event when everything goes from a regular monotonous moment to a possibly life-changing situation.

An example was when I was advised there was a blind man in front of a shelter who was refusing to leave. The man had been threatening other people and causing a disturbance. Upon my arrival, I saw an elderly man, sixtyish, sitting in front of the building with his legs crossed. He was wearing a backpack. He had a blindfold on with sunglasses over his eyes. He kind of looked like Willie Nelson. His hands were neatly on his lap. I said, "Sir, can I talk to you for a moment?" I was ignored. I said, "Sir, I am an officer with the police department. Can I speak with you for a moment?" I wanted him to come to me and to move away from the building because he was in the entryway. That would have been half the initial issue resolved. I approached this gentleman who appeared as if he was in a trance. I approached slowly because, to the best of my knowledge, he was blind, and I didn't want to startle him. I stooped down in front of the gentleman. I reached out and gently touched the man on his shoulder. With a speed that amazes me to this day, the man produced a scalpel from somewhere and swiped at my abdomen. I was barely able to move back in time to keep my intestines intact. My shirt was cleanly sliced just below my vest carrier. I was able to put the gentleman down quickly and place him in cuffs. He was an emotionally disturbed person (EDP), and the moment when the blade came out was the "oh shit" moment.

I put myself in a vulnerable position by getting too close with my knees bent as they were. I'm former military; therefore, my knees have seen their fair share of wear and tear. I shouldn't have underestimated this harmless-appearing fellow.

As a young police officer, an experienced criminal can pick you out of a lineup with ease. They will use phrases like: "This your first rodeo, huh?" They are letting you know that they know you are inexperienced. What they are really letting you know is they are dangerous. Information is power in almost every imaginable situation. Little things that we learn over time can build up a hell of an armory of reactive and proactive weapons.

Emotionally Disturbed Person

EDPs can be some of the saddest, funniest, most dangerous calls you can go on. As people in society, we tend to abide by a set of socially acceptable behaviors. Even when people veer away from those behaviors, it's usually not by a large leap. We can be assured that people will behave in a way that will protect at least that person's best interest. EDPs are inherently different. In some cases, they are not in control of themselves. Sometimes, they are in control, but just not to the degree we, as a society, are accustomed. There are different causes for these situations. It could be the person has a drug problem. It could be they have been injured, or perhaps they simply have a disability. Whatever the reason, police are not highly trained in psychology. My department provided a class to assist me in addressing EDPs. It was a weeklong class, 40 hours. It gave me a basic understanding of some of the many mental afflictions affecting the populace. Let's be honest. Psychologists go through years of training to deal with an EDP when he is relaxed and calm. My weeklong class was just enough to identify their may be a problem. As police officers, we are highly trained to deal with an array of issues. We are not experts in the field of EDPs. As a matter of fact, I would go so far as to say we are trained to deal with the exact opposite of an EDP. We give orders expecting them to be followed. How do you deal with someone who possibly doesn't understand or is too out of it to comprehend? As a rational person, I am not equipped to deal with an irrational situation because it would take me being irrational—not just irrational but an irrational state that's consistent with their irrational state.

In today's world, my response to an EDP is an even more difficult problem because the after actions review is done by the public. Compared to the world at large, we are experts simply by the number of times we have to deal with EDPs. When people who have no idea of the differences between a regular logical thinking person and an EDP watch an officer deal with one, it is not a winning proposition for the officer. When he gives the orders, and they are not answered as they should be, the officer will likely move on to the next course of action. When the public gets their review, they will have plenty of details the officer didn't have at the time. As a result, it will seem especially cruel for the police to have tased an autistic man for not following instructions. The biggest problem I would say is, people who are EDPs don't know they are EDPs. They don't identify themselves as EDPs, and that fact is just left out. There as a surprise for the officer to discover. There are many videos showing how civilians react as poorly as police officers during shooting scenarios. I would love to see a few with a surprise EDP.

There are times when the fact that a person is emotionally disturbed is painfully apparent. I had a call that had a family inside their residence watching TV. The interruption and reason for the call was a gentleman who dove Superman-style (horizontally through the air) through their front window landing in their living room. He was bleeding heavily and seemed surprised to see the family. He then ran to the back of the house and locked himself in a room. With this information given by the dispatcher, I was pretty aware this call was likely not to be a burglary and was more likely to be an EDP call. Fortunately, when we arrived, I didn't have to chase him, so we didn't end up in a foot pursuit. Unfortunately, we had to fight him to get him strapped down to get the medical and psychological help he needed. Emergency medical services (EMS) has a tough job, but they won't even come onto the scene until police say it's safe. That leaves police to deal with all the blood until such time as we can say it's "safe."

Fading

Every officer knows what fading is. It is the moment that precedes running. When you approach someone, and they start to fade, there is a gap of about one to six seconds before they run...or give up the idea. There are occasions when a moment of clarity has come upon a person, and they change their mind. Often, after this person is taken into custody and they calm down, they will tell you, "Hey man, I was about to run, but I changed my mind."

A fade can always be spotted if you are looking for it. When the person starts making space between you and him, that's a warning. Picture when you start an approach, and the person steps back in an effort to keep the car between you and him. It doesn't matter what he is saying. A person can fade while simultaneously appearing, to the untrained eye, to be completely cooperative. He could be saying, "Yes, sir. No problem," as he is still stepping backward. There are thousands of examples on social media, television shows and the like. A person will be saying, "Yes sir, officer. How can I help?" as they walk backward. Usually, an officer will advance in an effort to close the distance before the gap turns into a head start. He will close the distance in a manner that suits the situation. He may rush toward the person or slowly approach. If it's a truly hostile situation, the officer may "place hands" on the suspect immediately. Often, when we watch television, this is a point of confusion between civilians and police. There is a huge difference between cooperating and appearing to cooperate. If I say, for example, "Place your hands on the car, and you put your hand in your pocket while saying, "Yes sir, officer. No problem," that is noncompliance. To the civilian, of course, it may not seem like a big deal, but to an officer it's an "oh shit" moment.

How many times on *YouTube* or *Cops* have you seen someone fading? Look again. I'll bet you see a lot more examples. Also, check the videos in a lot of the controversial cases that have been in the media as of late. First, you listen to just the sounds. You will see quite often the persons are vocally compliant. After that first run, turn the sound off and watch it in silence. You will notice that your opinion of what happens may be altered drastically. A little bit of knowledge makes all the difference.

There is also a second kind of fading that a lot of officers are privy to; its "fading a call." This practice is a good way for the officer to lose his job. This is when an officer attempts to get the complainant not to file a police report. The officer wants to avoid the paperwork, so he tells the complainant the matter is not a big deal. This usually happens in petty situations like "My ex keeps calling me and hanging up." There is very little filing a police report will do to remedy this matter. The police officer still has to write a multi-page report about this matter. The report still has to be approved by supervisors. I have never heard of someone fading a call of a serious nature, but I'm certain it happens.

The major danger in fading a call, even a minor one, is that the major calls start somewhere. Yes, that guy taking a bat to his girlfriend's head often didn't need a jumping-off point. Sometimes though, it starts with a couple of phone calls. If a minor call that an officer has faded turns into a major call, there is no CYA (cover your ass) that's going to save his job.

Foot Pursuits

Officers need to keep a situation under control for obvious and not so obvious reasons. Perhaps we don't want to leave a scene unattended, which would happen if we get involved in a foot pursuit. Perhaps we don't want the suspect to have an opportunity to drop something that is needed for the case. Perhaps we just don't want to end up in a foot pursuit. As a rookie officer, I didn't mind foot pursuits. As a senior, more heavily seasoned as well as heavier officer, I mind a bit more. The bottom line is that if you see someone is about to run, the officer will try to stop it before it happens. The "fade" is a well-tested indicator the suspect is about to run.

A well-known term is one that I have previously mentioned, "foot pursuit." A foot pursuit is a simple statement that is self-explanatory. When suspects run, we chase them. Sometimes, we are not in vehicles. I have mentioned that, as a rookie, I didn't mind a foot pursuit. I actually enjoyed the rush. There is nothing more satisfying than having it being displayed in no uncertain terms that you are the better man. Say what? Yes, police have egos too! I have worked out for months during the academy. I have been trained. I have pushed myself harder than my classmates. I have put in extra hours. I would like to know it was not for nothing. When I pull up on a vehicle and that vehicle stops abruptly. I'm on alert. When that driver-side door opens up so fast that it often is ajar before the car stops, I'm on alert. I have seen it a hundred times. I know that if that door opens before the vehicle stops, it is likely the door will bounce back and knock the driver off balance as he jumps out of the car. That's an advantage. The problem that often comes up is that sometimes, the person does not care about stopping the vehicle before he gets out. That means the officer has to deal with the public safety issue before beginning the foot pursuit.

The pursuit itself is extremely dangerous. Perhaps the suspect knows the area. Perhaps he drove to the area just for that reason. What happens when he runs into a backyard with a dog? What happens when he runs into a dark backyard with a low-hanging clothesline? (This happened to me.) What if he hits a corner and waits to ambush me? (This also happened to me.)

That's only the bare surface of the difficulty of a foot pursuit. It is difficult for the average person to tell north, south, east, and west. Imagine having to do it while running. The officer is responsible for calling out his location and direction of travel. It is not a rule; it's a lifesaving directive. If you are running after someone and get into trouble, help is not coming if they don't know where you are.

There is also the ability to fight after a 200-yard sprint, and yes, I said fight. Not much changes in the way of the suspect's feelings about going to jail after a foot pursuit. He still doesn't want to go to jail. Often, he will turn and fight. The thing is, when they turn and fight after a long run, I'm tired. The officer is at a clear disadvantage. The officer has 35 pounds of extra gear on him at all times. I truly have no idea how we ever catch anyone. We catch guys who are wearing basketball shorts and tennis shoes. That aside, when we catch them, we have to get the cuffs on them.

You have to know, most times, if they had a weapon, they don't anymore. While this is not the most common reason people run, it has to be in the top five. They need time to get rid of whatever they had. They hit a corner and throw whatever they had so the officer can't find the item, and so they never had it. These are the people that when you catch them, they say, "I give. I give." They will usually go into cuffs pretty easy.

You've got the guys who leave whatever they had in the car. These guys have no intention of being caught; they will run their hardest. They are trying to separate themselves from whatever is in that car. They are trying to run and get out of your sight. They are trying to get to a place where they can say, "I was never in that car; you've made a mistake." These people will usually go willingly because they are victims of mistaken identity. They are certain that this whole "misunderstanding" will be sorted out in due time.

There is a small group of people who will run from the police during a traffic stop for little or no reason. These people are hopped up on adrenaline. They will run for a short while and give up almost immediately. They ran simply because they were afraid. They may have a suspended license or a minor infraction that caused them to make a bad decision.

Then, there are those who have warrants. They know that if they get caught, they are definitely going to jail. Some of them know they are going to jail for an extended amount of time. They tend to be the ones who run until they can't run anymore. After what is often a very lengthy run, they turn. They will ambush you. They will turn a corner and stop. When you follow and turn that same corner, they will attack. Now, let me say, officers know, or they should know, to turn corners cautiously and wide. Officers don't always do this. Whether it's because they are a rookie and haven't learned this precaution yet or are simply tired and not thinking straight, it's a deadly mistake. If you were set to spend an extended time in prison, how hard would you fight to stay free? People fight in different ways. You may choose to fight in court. Some people choose to fight on the street and in the moment. You had better be prepared. You are fighting to take someone into custody. You are trying to arrest this suspect, who is one of several suspects you've arrested this week. This is Wednesday for you. For him, this is the day that will play back in his mind for years to come. He is going to give it his all. He doesn't have to hold anything in reserve. He is fighting for his freedom, which makes him extremely dangerous. You had better be certain that after the foot pursuit, you've got something left in the tank. You had better be certain that you don't think you are fighting to take this person into custody. You better be totally aware that you are fighting for your life. After it's over and you have won, I hope you have even more left because you now have to fight to defend your actions.

Cluster

Another term universally known is cluster. The full term is cluster f**k. This is when a case becomes more complicated than it originally appeared. The most mundane call can turn out to be a cluster. The speed at which a regular call can turn into a cluster is surprising.

When you go out to a simple call like an alarm, and it turns into a burglary involving the neighbors, that's a cluster. I once had an alarm call that sent me to a person's house. Upon checking out the alarm, I spoke with the homeowner. She advised she had set off the alarm upon returning home. A simple mistake, right? Well, while I was at the residence, I saw the lady had two of everything. I'm not talking about two end tables. I'm talking, two couches and two TVs. The lady had four lamps and two coffee tables. This was weird, to say the least. On a hunch, I checked to see if there had been any burglaries in the area. It turns out the next-door residence had had a burglary. Apparently, the homeowner had a relative who was sick out of town. She had gone to live with the relative to take care of them until they were better (how noble). The neighbor had come home just to check on her house. When she arrived, she found that her house had been cleaned out, completely cleaned out.

Of course, to the civilian, this would seem like a simple matter. The bad guy is right next door. Arrest the suspect, give the stuff back to the victim, and be done. Not so simple. A consent to search form must be signed by the person who, as a result, will be arrested. Usually, they won't sign (I wouldn't either). She wouldn't, so a warrant had to be written. The warrant needs to be written to get into the residence and verify the stuff inside the residence is actually the stolen items. It could be the woman is just eccentric. A search warrant has to be signed by a judge. This was not during normal working hours for the judges, so you have to contact the duty judge and go out to his residence for him to sign. The only probable cause I have is my word, which says I saw something that a reasonable person would deem suspicious having seen the items and the description given of the items in the original burglary report.

Fortunately, for me, we have a burglary division. The burglary division came out and took over the case. I was on this case for about nine hours before I was able to clear. I work a ten-hour shift, and I was already eight hours into my shift. This call wound up being a cluster.

Who, Me?

One of the most common giveaways when someone is lying or about to lie is when you ask them a direct question, and they respond with an indirect answer. The most common occurrence is any question answered with the question: "Who, me?" Any officer is going to listen to the rest of your statement with skepticism. If I ask you, "Were you inside that residence when we arrived?" and your answer is, "Who, me?" you did it. Now, realistically, that doesn't mean you are lying, but it does mean that you are stalling for time. It's the same thing when your spouse asks you, "Did you eat the piece of cake I was saving?" and you respond, "Who, me?" Same principle.

Other Notable Terms

Non-life-threatening: This is an ambiguous term meaning a serious wound that the victim is not expected to die from. It is ambiguous because doctors are unlikely to give the diagnosis. The non-life-threatening caveat usually comes from those who are not qualified to give it, such as the police.

Cover your ass (CYA): This is action the officer takes to make his actions and the reasons for his actions clear. For example, if you tase someone in a totally justified situation, do the report in detail immediately. If that person goes to the hospital later that night for unrelated issues and dies, that report needs to be in. Anything you type after the fact will seem like an attempt to cover something up. Good supervisors are keen on CYA. Their job is to make sure you don't make any of the mistakes they made as a young officer. To the young officer, this means a lot of extra reports and extra details in those extra reports.

5

Drug Dealer vs. Peace Officer

Being an officer is hard. Being an officer in uniformed patrol is even harder. We now have cameras and recorders built into everything. The problem with that is it's almost impossible to train the public to think like an officer when they are inclined to think as a civilian. What I mean by that is when I approach a situation, I have to assess it the way it is. When you speak to a Chinese man, and he doesn't speak English, you have to speak in Chinese if you want him to understand. At the risk of sounding politically incorrect, I think if someone is speaking irately, upset, hateful, or ignorantly, you have to speak that language as well. I am speaking from experience. In most cases, cooler heads prevail, but sometimes you need to yell, "Put your hands on the fucking car," at the same volume they are so they can hear you.

Hindsight is twenty-twenty. Civilians can look back at a situation for weeks and months to determine what was done right or wrong. Officers deal with situations as they arise. We don't always make the right decisions. We make our decisions based mainly on our personal experience. I have been shaped by my experience over time. While gathering that experience, I've made many mistakes that I won't make again.

Sometime between 2005-2006, I was working an area that we

shall call Dalton Estates. This area was known for its many apartment complexes, most of which were low-income efficiency apartments. This was a violent area and was known for shootings and disturbances. What made this area even more dangerous was, like most poor places, it was cheap to live there—the times being what they were, and Hurricane Katrina had just occurred. This was a city in Louisiana that was only about 45 minutes north of New Orleans. A lot of people who were displaced by the storm moved there.

At this time, I was still considered a rookie officer (under three years) working in the uniformed patrol division. I was dispatched to a case that involved an apartment that had five bullet holes in the door. Upon my arrival, I saw the apartment was an upstairs apartment near the stairwell. I could clearly see that the bullet holes appeared to have originated from a weapon that had to have been manned from the top or near the top of the stairs. I approached the door with caution even though I had been advised the scene was code four (safe). I spoke with the complainant, an elderly woman who advised me a drug dealer had shot at her residence. The victim advised that she had five children who were in the residence at the time. The victim, we will call her Ms. Angela, said she had a son who was not currently at the residence. She said that her son had a drug problem. Ms. Angela said that her son, Ricky, bought a dime rock from a local drug dealer. Ricky gave the drug dealer eight dollars for a ten-dollar rock with the promise to pay an additional ten dollars the following day. On the following day, Ricky paid the drug dealer eight more dollars to clear the debt. The dealer advised the deal was an additional ten dollars. The dealer advised he wanted the full ten the following day.

Ricky decided this was an unfair situation, so he opted not to pay. After Ricky did not show up the following day to pay, the drug dealer began to send threats to Ricky's house by way of neighbors and neighborhood folk. As could be expected, Ricky did not respond or get back in touch with the drug dealer. Having a reputation to uphold, the drug dealer went to Ricky's apartment and shot into the door. The door was hit at an angle, so the bullets entered the door on the right side and exited the door leftward bound and striking a nearby wall. Because the wall was adjacent to another apartment, the bullets entered into that apartment as well, where they came to a stop.

At the time of the incident, there were multiple children in this apartment. The children called Ms. Angela, who was not at home at the time of the shooting; Ms. Angela then called the police. In walked this fairly new officer, badge gleaming, leather all shiny, there to help. Ms. Angela advised him of the train of events, which the officer took note of on his hand pad. The officer took down the description of the suspect. Ms. Angela advised her son, Ricky, had been sent to a distant town with some relatives for his own safety. The new officer knocked on the neighbor's doors to survey the damage and to ask if anyone had seen this incident take place. Had anyone seen this drug dealer come and shoot into this residence multiple times? Perhaps someone had seen a vehicle leave the area at the time of the shooting. The officer was unable to locate one witness who saw anything. The officer then contacted the manager of the apartment complex because he noticed there were cameras on the property. Upon speaking with the manager, he found the cameras had not worked in years, and the manager kept them up for show. The manager even went so far as to tell the police officer not to tell the tenants the cameras did not work. Cameras that didn't work, no casings on scene and no witnesses, needless to say, this case was coming to a dead-end pretty quickly. Ms. Angela was pretty certain who had shot into her residence and even the reason why. Ms. Angela did not know the drug dealer's name, but she had given a pretty good description.

The new officer with the gleaming badge scoured the neighborhood for someone who fit the description given by Ms. Angela. The officer was unable to find this dealer.

Lo and behold, Ms. Angela contacted the police and said the drug dealer whom she was certain shot into her residence was currently in her apartment complex parking lot and had just locked eyes with her. The new officer with the gleaming badge was dispatched and quickly made his way to the apartment complex to find the drug dealer in the parking lot. Upon seeing the officer, the dealer immediately tried to fade. As the officer approached in a marked unit, the drug dealer took a few steps back until he disappeared into the alleyway of the apartment complex. Fortunately, the officer knew the area. The officer knew the area so well, in fact, that he knew the path the drug dealer would take. The officer had taken this path many times. The officer with the gleaming badge had actually lived in this apartment complex. The officer quickly exited his vehicle and went around the building to the point where the officer expected the dealer to exit. A few moments later, the dealer ran into the officer almost literally because the drug dealer was running while looking backward.

Feeling pretty good, the officer took the drug dealer into custody, placed handcuffs on him and walked him to the car. The officer with the gleaming badge searched the drug dealer and found nothing. Still in contact with the victim via phone, dispatch advised the officer the victim confirmed he had the right person. The officer contacted other officers so they could watch the dealer while he checked the path the drug dealer had taken for drugs or a firearm. The officer with the shiny leather gear found a little baggy in a drain with a half-ounce of crack cocaine. The drug dealer was read his rights per Miranda and asked about the drugs. The drug dealer asked why the police were harassing him, as he had nothing on him. The drug dealer advised he had just been standing outside waiting for a friend. When the officer told the drug dealer the drugs had been located, the dealer advised he wanted his lawyer. This statement effectively ended the conversation between the officer and the suspect.

Feeling quite proud of himself, the officer brought the dealer to the district and commenced booking him into prison. Well, the rookie officer had to get his probable cause signed by a supervisor, which was a sergeant or above. The probable cause is the reason and justification the officer has to relieve a citizen of his freedom written out in legal and lawful terms. Upon turning in this probable cause to the lieutenant, the officer was advised immediately that he had no probable cause. The victim had advised that she had never seen the shooter. The person who had had the initial deal, Ricky, was currently out of town and unreachable. The drugs that had been located in a drain along the path the dealer had taken, had not been found on his person and, therefore, could not be put in his possession for certain. The dealer was to be released immediately.

The officer learned a few lessons from this incident. He learned that once the suspect is out of sight, you cannot account for what he has done or is doing. The officer got a better understanding of probable cause and what is required to achieve it. While the lessons proved invaluable for his future years in the department, it did little to fix the current situation.

The dealer, now extremely relieved and excited, did not leave humbly, as one would expect after narrowly missing some serious jail time on a technicality. The dealer became belligerent, cursing and proclaiming that he was untouchable. The officer released the dealer and humbly apologized for the inconvenience.

After the release of the dealer, the lieutenant took the officer aside and explained a few things to the officer about not being able to "win them all" and how people who are bad don't stop because they got a break. After the conversation, the officer received a counseling statement, which stated the officer required more training. The officer did not, however, receive more training. This was a CYA action on the part of the lieutenant.

In most cases, this is the end. There is usually nothing more to the story.

Officers don't tend to hold grudges, not because they are simply above such pettiness, but more because of the simple volume of things they have to deal with. Given enough time, this particular drug dealer's face would blend into the multitude of faces the officer had to deal with on a daily basis. If you've ever seen someone you know to be an officer because you've seen him in uniform and he has seen you, be aware. He may not know you or remember you. He may only know you as a familiar face, nothing more. He does, however, tend to be on guard because he recognizes that he has seen you before and does not remember from where. In my own situation, I grew up in the city where I police, so I'm at a particular loss. I don't know if I remember you from high school or some incident as a police officer.

As I said, this particular drug dealer was anything but grateful for my mistake or his benefit as a result. I would see him almost every day, and he would see me. He yelled obscenities at me and grabbed his crotch over and over again. I would not stop or approach him because I knew that anything I did, no matter how warranted, would simply look like some sort of retaliation. So, I would simply endure this drug dealer yelling at me all sorts of things as I passed by.

When this new officer with the shiny badge started working the streets, the buzz phrase was community policing. This is supposed to mean, as a police officer, you are bonding with your assigned community. In theory, this looks like a police officer jumping rope with some kids on the corner or perhaps helping an old lady get her bags out of the car and walking them to the door. In actuality, it's going to community meetings and having the community leaders tell you where the problems are and what you need to do to fix them. The new police officer with the gleaming badge was taking his duties very seriously. The officer would spend a large bit of his time outside of his vehicle, actually speaking with people and walking through apartment complexes. One day very soon after the last incident, the officer (me) was speaking with an apartment manager. The manager was telling me the issues she had and that she would like more patrols. This was normal. They all wanted more police in the area. It was simply better for business. The manager asked to show me the areas where the kids would gather and smoke marijuana. As with all good marijuana smoking spots, it was far from the office and in a hidden spot on the grounds. As I walked with the manager to this secret place, I saw the drug dealer, and he saw me. I looked as he clearly sized me up. He looked me first in the eyes and then down to my feet and back up to my eyes. (We call this a check.) This was not unexpected because the drug dealer gave me much attention as I passed him on the street. This particular time I was on foot and with the apartment manager. I didn't want any trouble, and I assumed he didn't want any either. I was mistaken. The drug dealer said, "Who the f*** you eyeballing?" I was flustered for more than one reason. First, I'm Webalization, a man who has earned his respect. Second, I'm a police officer in uniform, and this petty drug dealer has the audacity to speak to me in such a negative tone. Remembering I was in the presence of the apartment manager, I told him "Hey, find another place to be or I will find a reason to arrest you."

With that, I simply continued on my previous course with the manager as if I had not been disrespected. As we walked, the manager told me that he did not live there and that he was a drug dealer. She said that he sold drugs to the tenants in D building. I asked her if she would like him removed. She advised she would. Once the manager had shown me the area where she had found children smoking more than once, she asked if I would check on the area often. I told her I would, and we headed back to the office, where I had parked my unit.

Upon my arrival back to my unit, what do I see? The drug dealer is leaned up against my unit on the phone. The drug dealer is on the phone with the internal affairs division of my department. He is, in a loud, obnoxious tone, telling them that I had told him only moments ago that I would plant some drugs on him to put him in jail. I also noticed that he had a small group of people forming around my vehicle. I told the drug dealer to get off my car. He responded, "F*** you." I had reached my limit. There is a charge on the books that prohibits the use of vulgar language in public. I approached the drug dealer and told him to put his hands behind his back. The drug dealer ignored me and began to yell on the phone that I was harassing him now. I again told him to put his hands behind his back. The drug dealer refused and began to walk off. It was at this point that I grabbed his hand in an effort to put handcuffs on him. The drug dealer then attempted to run. It was too late. I had a hold of him. The drug dealer was of small stature, and I figured I could easily get him under control. Still, I decided I would call for back up as soon as I had the opportunity. At this point, the drug dealer realized that he had taken it too far and was in a full-fledged attempt to run. I had a good grip and was holding tight. I was working him into position to do a straight-arm bar takedown (per defensive tactics) when one of the previous bystanders intervened. The person who intervened was a woman who was obviously in the late stages of pregnancy. At this point, I would say I had control of the drug dealer's left arm. The woman, in an attempt to force me to let the drug dealer go, wrapped her arm around his and mine. At the same time, the drug dealer was using this opportunity to pry my fingers loose. My concern was both not losing my suspect and not hurting this woman who was clearly at least seven to eight months pregnant. The fact that I was now pulling back as not to hurt this woman caused me to loosen my grip on the drug dealer, and, as a group, we have moved out of the center of the complex and into a corridor of apartments. It is at this time I manage to have one hand free so that I may call for assistance. I called out my location trying my best to sound calm and called for assistance. Calmly, I asked that that assistance be prompt. At this early time in my career, I didn't want to make an "officer in distress call." The crowd, which had only been increasing since the initial encounter, continued to grow steadily. By the time I managed to call for assistance, it had gotten out of hand. This was once a neighborhood I knew. I had spent years in this neighborhood. A lot of the residents knew me by first name. Due to the influx of people from New Orleans as a result of the flood, I looked into the crowd and could not recognize a familiar face. All I did see was a large crowd surrounding me in the small hallway. It was at this point someone grabbed the hand-cuffs out of my hand. People in the crowd were pushing me and pulling the drug dealer. I could feel people punching me in the back. This entire encounter felt like it took forever. After what seemed like ten minutes, I found myself in front of one of the apartments. The door was open, and the drug dealer was trying to go in. I was holding on to the door thinking my backup must be near. I took out my second pair of handcuffs, still intent on arresting this guy. I then noticed that he actually had a hold of me and was pulling me into this apartment. This moment instilled me with fear. It was the first time in this entire incident that I could say that I was not nervous but actually afraid. What did he have in mind? What did he think, dragging me into the apartment? Until this point, I had decided not to draw my weapon. I decided that with the crowd in such close contact the safest place for my weapon was in the holster. I decided that if I was drug into the apartment, then all bets were off. I decided that I would draw my weapon and fire. I decided I was not going into the apartment. This was a very scary situation, as my options were disappearing fast. The crowd was pushing me into the apartment. I started to fight; I started to fight hard. I was already exhausted from this encounter that was lasting way longer than I had planned. I heard sirens in the background, but they appeared to have been going the wrong way, passing me up. I managed to get my second pair of handcuffs on the drug dealer's left arm. Unfortunately, now the tables had turned. I began to punch. It is not the policy of the police department to "punch" suspects. It is in my experience that when in real moments of fear, anger and panic we revert to the tactics we know best. You would think it's the tactics I learned in the police department, perhaps what I had learned in the army. Nope. I reverted to what I had learned in the schoolyard. The drug dealer had my left hand. With my right hand, I punched him in the first vulnerable spot that presented itself, his left ear. His head was caught between my fist and the wall. I presume his head hit a stud. As you know, a stud does not give way. Energy, kinetic or otherwise, is never lost. The force came back to me instantly, sending a shocking pain through my hand and into my shoulder. The entire time I had been fighting, I was in the doorway, attempting to hold onto the doorframe to keep from going into the apartment. The option to retreat that I had neglected just moments prior had been taken away by the crowd as they moved forward toward me. As I stood there, my shoulder in pain, I was at a loss. This had never happened before. At the time, I hadn't even truly known what I had done, how I was injured. I only knew I was in pain and this was a new factor in my dilemma. WHERE IS THAT

BACKUP! The drug dealer and I both fell to the floor inside the apartment after a huge push from the crowd. The door slammed shut! As far as I knew, we two were the only ones in the apartment. I immediately went to grab for my weapon as I had initially planned. To my almost tear-worthy disappointment, I could not. My arm was barely responding to my commands. The three-action holster, which until this point had kept my weapon safe, was now imprisoning my salvation. The fine motor skills of my fingers were gone.

The drug dealer almost immediately got up and tried to run down the hall. I immediately grabbed his legs, causing him to fall again. I was in trouble. I had no use of my weapon. I was now holding onto the drug dealer's legs to keep him away from whatever he was trying to get. It was at this moment I chose to think that my only charge is vulgar language in public. I thought, *Where did I mess up?* I thought, *WHERE IS MY BACK UP?!*

I'm on the floor, holding onto a pair of legs for dear life. The drug dealer is now kicking me. I'm having the hardest time holding onto his feet because he has turned over onto his back and now has leverage. The right side of my body is in pain. I try to hold on, but my grip is weak. I can grab repeatedly but cannot hold on. I manage to get to my pepper spray knowing full well that we are in an enclosed area, and the tight space will cause both of us to be unable to see. I spray the dealer in and around his face. Just as I thought, the spray immediately fills the room, making it hard to breathe. When the spray hits my eyes, they start to water and close. Having gotten the worst of it, the drug dealer stops moving away and attacks me. This is a relief. I would rather fight him in my current condition than deal with him with a weapon. He attacks me. We fight. I hold on until the door bursts open. The cavalry had arrived.

Multiple uniformed officers storm through the door. I can

see, barely, a line of people laid down on the ground, hands on their head, and fingers interlocked just outside of the door. Officers had to disperse a crown before they could get to me. This situation was really a bad one that could have been much worse. Officers immediately took the drug dealer into custody.

I was asked if I needed an ambulance. I told them no. I got up and dusted myself off. I straightened my gear out. I made sure my belt buckle aligned with my seam. I secured all of my pins and made sure my pouches were snapped shut. I still had no idea what was wrong with my shoulder, as this had never happened before. I ignored the pain and walked out of the apartment. I did my absolute best to look nonchalant, so the people who were around didn't see that I was injured. I didn't want them to see my weakness. I didn't want them to know they hurt me. I very calmly walked to my unit, got in and drove to the district.

The pregnant female was also located and arrested. She was the girlfriend of the drug dealer.

I had my shoulder dislocated. It had to be placed back into the socket. A dislocated shoulder is a permanent injury. It's a permanent injury because the shoulder is more inclined to "pop" out of the socket once it has before. I was assigned "light duty" for six weeks. When an officer is on light duty, he is not allowed to work "extra duty."

A quick note on extra duty: Not always, but in most cases, police are underpaid for what they do. If a person has a dangerous job, it's truly not worth it if he can't provide a decent life for his family. A decent life requires money. Extra duty details are how the police officer balances the budget. An extra duty usually pays at least the officer's overtime rate and often more. The extra duty is usually an easier job than his regular job. The main caveat is the officer must work his regular schedule if he wishes to work extra duty as well.

Like most officers, I made quite a bit of money working extra duties. To me, six weeks of light duty meant at least an 1800-dollar monthly reduction in pay. The extra duty, whatever it may be, still goes on without you. There is a possibility that you may lose your detail permanently. This means I'm short a lot of money that I once had. So, if I had a family at the time, I would have been in a world of hurt financially. If any of you are married, you know a sure-fire way to have an argument with your wife is having money problems. A veteran officer may avoid any altercation that could risk him being injured. I find that not being prepared to engage or hesitant to engage in a physical altercation is even more dangerous.

What did we learn? As a rookie officer, I made plenty of mistakes. Mistakes are to be expected, but only once. I could point out the mistakes from the beginning. I could point out the tactical errors, but that's not the biggest mistake I made. After I released the drug dealer and I passed him in the street, he would yell and scream, etc. At the time, I deemed this annoying but ultimately harmless. What was actually happening was the drug dealer was being emboldened. The more I let him "slide," the more hyped he became. What should I have done? What could I have done? First, I shouldn't have allowed him to get to the point where he had the gall to "check me."

Police are always said to be harassing people. We do. Any unwanted contact will be defined as harassing. That's nature. As I have said many times, the drug dealer was a drug dealer. I am not speaking of the "he has been convicted in court of selling drugs" scenario. I am speaking of the fact that it was common knowledge that he was a drug dealer. I should have come into contact with him at every opportunity. If I am in contact with him, he can't do business. Perhaps he would have left the area if I made it "too hot." The neighborhood would have been better off without one extra drug dealer.

Mistakes and errors in judgment:

When he contacted me in the apartment complex, I should have attempted to arrest him immediately. I know it would seem I didn't have a valid charge, but the manager didn't want him there. That's more than sufficient to have him removed.

At any time during this whole altercation, I could have disengaged. I could have let the drug dealer go and caught him another day. Officers tend to forget they do have the ability to retreat. When I felt like the situation was getting out of hand, nothing was preventing me from simply letting him go.

The biggest and most costly mistake I made was the failure to respond properly to resistance. When I initially decided to take the drug dealer into custody, I should have been…more aggressive. The minute he resisted, I should have been less tolerant. He should not have been allowed to take any steps after I had his arm. I should have used every ounce of effort I could muster to get him to the ground. In reference to the female who interfered, I could have ended this a lot sooner. The drug dealer would have been in custody had it not been for the pregnant woman who interfered. She obstructed justice, which is a charge. At the time, I did everything I could do not to injure her. That was not my responsibility. Like anyone, I do not want to injure a pregnant woman. The child she carries is an innocent. It is not the child's fault the mother decides to place herself, and by proxy the child, in danger. However, my life is precious as well. Do I allow this woman's bad decision to place my life in danger? At the time, I was single. Today, I am married with children of my own. Without hesitation, I will put myself in harm's way to protect a child, a woman or the average citizen. I will not, however, allow my children to go without a father or my wife to be a widow in an effort

to protect any one of these individuals from their own poor decisions.

6

Hand on Firearm/Unintended Intimidation

I can't tell you how many times I have been standing around on some detail, minding my business, when someone asked me why my hand was on my gun. Simple answer: the gun belt is in the way of my pockets. It's uncomfortable to put my hands in my pockets, not to mention unsafe. Most times, this has nothing to do with you. Stop being so full of yourself.

7

Difficult Decision Made on Providence Street

I swear, some days it is better to just stay in bed. While working in the violent crimes office as a general detective, I received a call about a victim having suffered a single gunshot wound to the back. The department receives hundreds of calls like this one. There are always people who have disagreements. It's my job to go out and find out what happened. I have to go and piece the details of the event back together and see who has done the ill deed. It's my job to see who has broken the law. I have to locate those individuals and present them to be judged. I have a large pool of resources at my disposal to accomplish this task. These resources are also my responsibility. Their actions take place as a direct result of my orders and the information I provide. They depend on me to give them consistent and credible information on which they will act in good faith. What happens when I have the information to act, but it's not absolute? Who makes the decision to act? Who is going to be the one who suffers the consequence of a bad decision?

I went to the call like any other. The victim was transported to the hospital with a non-life-threatening gunshot wound to the back. It turns out there had been a shooting in the parking lot involving multiple people, and the bullet had gone through a wall, striking the victim in the back. The victim, an innocent person, had not seen anyone. The initial responding officer was already in the area when the call went out. The officer had been at a nearby apartment working another case when he heard multiple gunshots and responded. The officer told me he had seen a male juvenile running from the direction of the gunfire only moments after he'd heard the gunfire. The officer could not say if the juvenile was the shooter or if he was simply running from those who were shooting. The officer advised he was certain the juvenile ran into apartment twenty-eight. The officer said that a female was behind the juvenile, but the juvenile closed the door behind himself, slamming the door in the face of the female juvenile. The officer told me he could not be certain of the circumstance, as he was still clearing the scene. While processing the scene, we received two anonymous tips stating the people who had just been shooting were located in apartment twenty-eight. The anonymous tipster advised they did not see the people actually go into the apartment this time, but advised they had seen the people who were shooting and knew them to hang out in apartment twenty-eight. The anonymous tip advised there were multiple juveniles who varied in age, and they all most likely ran into that apartment. The anonymous tipster advised the juveniles sold drugs from the apartment, and that might have been what the shooting was about.

I spoke with the female juvenile who said that she had just come from walking across town and that she tried to run into a stranger's apartment because people were shooting. Reasonable, right? Being the female was a juvenile, we contacted a parent to come out. Upon the arrival of the parent, we found out the female lived nearby, and the male who had run into the apartment was her stepbrother. The girl confirmed the juvenile male was in the apartment. The girl said there were other juveniles in the apartment as well and possibly a toddler. This was not her apartment, nor did she know whose apartment it was. I knocked on the door repeatedly (which was obviously dangerous), but no one would come to the door. There were no lights on that were visible through the windows. I had the mother give me her son's number and attempted to call him. I was unable to get an answer. I had the mother call and still no answer. The mother texted him the police were outside, and he needed to come out. There was an immediate reply of "No."

Did this mean the juvenile was inside the apartment? No. Did this mean he knew the police were outside of the residence? This juvenile could simply be playing a practical joke on his mother. Was the person responding actually her son? These were the questions that were still present and important.

Considering the anonymous tips and the fact the officer advised he had seen a juvenile run into apartment twenty-eight, I deemed I had probable cause to get a search warrant for the residence. In these situations, the special weapons and tactics (SWAT) team would be called in to clear the residence for a search.

It's not certain, but it's a possibility a judge would have signed the search warrant. We would then have legal authority to enter the residence. My dilemma was I was certain that at least some of the people inside the apartment were juveniles. I was fairly certain, or as certain as I could be, there were guns inside the residence. There was also the possibility there were drugs, not to mention a toddler inside the residence. With all of this information, SWAT would be necessary to enter the residence.

SWAT teams make dynamic entries and make quick decisions necessary in tactical entry situations. If they see a person with a gun aimed at them, there is really no question which of the two, suspect or officer, will survive. Unlike often seen on television, there are no leg shots. The targets we practice to shoot have no arms or legs. Center mass is where we are taught to shoot. The best of us (SWAT) are even better at this.

Coming back to point, if SWAT had to make an entry there was no doubt the juveniles would be in danger. There was even a good possibility a juvenile would be killed. The juveniles were stupid enough not to come outside while the building was surrounded. They were stupid enough not to come outside even with their mother advising them of that fact. I was certain they would not remain still as SWAT made entry.

This was my problem. I was the lead detective, and everyone was looking to me to make the decision upon which all uniformed officers would act. Do I send SWAT into the building when I know this would most likely end in the death of one or more juveniles? Do I break down the perimeter and say I do not have enough probable cause to warrant the search? This would mean I'd be letting the kids who have guns and have shown they are willing to use them out in the world, thus, giving them the chance to hurt someone else. Was there anyone else in the apartment? Could I even be certain the text came from inside the apartment? No one else on scene would give any input, and why would they? I wouldn't. Who would want to put their name in the headlines the following day?

I broke the scene down. I advised uniformed patrol that it was over. I'm still waiting to see if I made the right decision.

8

That Time I Was Sued

Every officer has learned at one time or another that doing the right thing isn't always doing the right thing. I've heard this contradictory statement before but never knew what it meant. I am a police officer for all the right reasons. I became a police officer to make a difference in my community. I have my personal prejudices, but none of the really bad ones (I don't like bullies). I wasn't beaten up in school and became an officer to get revenge. I don't get off on having power over people. If I go into every situation with the best intentions and keep my training in mind, I can't go wrong...right?

There is a common statement made in many police departments, that states, "If you ain't getting sued, you ain't doing your job." I've learned that getting sued is sometimes unavoidable unless you don't do your job.

Being sued means you may have wronged someone in some fashion, and they have taken legal action to seek correction, usually through financial means. Many people can be financially ruined if they are sued and found liable for an amount as little as 10,000 dollars.

Sometime in my early years, I was working the Dalton Estates area. I was in uniformed patrol. A big part of uniformed patrol is community policing. I would routinely go into the apartment complexes and speak with the people. I was well known in my neighborhood. I was well-liked by the older people. The younger people didn't hate me.

One day, I was working the area just like any other day. I was handling a call in an adjacent apartment complex when a call went out about a stabbing that occurred in Woodside's Edge apartment. This was sent out as a code three call (an emergency requiring immediate action). I was advised by dispatch there was a victim in building seventeen who was in a fight, possibly with a roommate. I was advised there was a knife involved, and someone had been stabbed. The dispatcher was having trouble getting more information due to circumstances. Being right next door, I arrived on the scene almost immediately. I had no description of the suspect.

Upon my arrival at the apartment complex, I saw there were plenty of people out and about. As I approached building seventeen, I saw a slender male exiting the building. He had two hands full of clothes. He wore shorts and a wife-beater (a sleeveless undershirt). The male made it past the walkway and was on the side of my vehicle before I could exit. He was walking pretty fast. I spoke to the guy, "Sir, can I speak with you for a moment?" He said, "Why?" and kept walking. He seemed upset. I got out of my unit and said, "Sir, I just need to talk to you for just a moment." I approached the male, and he answered, "WHY?" in the most aggressive tone. I could see that he was hostile. I approached him and said please, but it was too late. He had dropped his clothes and balled up his fist.

I paused in my mind for only a moment to assess what I was seeing. I saw a male with his clothes in his hands, leaving his apartment. I saw a male who appeared angry because he maybe just got into an argument with his lady. Perhaps she kicked him out, and this was why he had his clothes in hand. I also saw a male who has reacted in an extreme manner that was both unprovoked and unwarranted for the situation. Also, as far as I knew, there was someone in the apartment bleeding from being stabbed, and they needed help.

As I approached the male, he had his fist balled up as if he was going to hit me. I felt that I didn't have time for this, but I approached him slowly. I told him, "I'm investigating a stabbing." At the same time, I slowly grabbed his hand. He jerked his hand away. I immediately slammed him to the ground. When I say slammed, I mean, I put him down fast. This was one of the few times where I was able to use the academy training verbatim. I took him down using the straight-arm bar takedown. He actually landed in the grass. He was a lightweight person, maybe 160 pounds, so it was easy to place him into cuffs. I don't know if it was his light weight or the fact that I thought someone could be in the apartment dying. Regardless, I was able to get the male into cuffs pretty quickly. I placed him in the back of my unit secured as other officers started to arrive. I went to apartment four per the dispatcher. In apartment four, I found a victim suffering from a single knife wound to the abdomen and the suspect who stabbed him in the apartment. The wound was not that bad, a single stab wound to the abdomen with a small knife approximately three inches long. The knife didn't hit any arteries and basically just bled. EMS did not transport the victim to the hospital. The victim decided they would get a ride themselves and save the money. I arrested the suspect. Someone else transported the suspect to the district so that I could deal with other matters. The male had nothing to do with the entire situation.

I went back to my vehicle and, lo and behold, the male was extremely upset and irate. He was spouting off plenty of stuff about my parents and poor breeding. I brought the male to the front of my unit, in front of the camera. I took his cuffs off and apologized. I attempted to explain what happened. The male, of course, did not want to hear what I had to say and told me he wanted by name and badge number. I gave him the information he wanted. I allowed him to speak with my supervisor, who was currently on scene. My supervisor apologized and attempted to explain what had happened. He was promptly cursed out as well. The camera footage was downloaded to show the male had no injuries and seemed fine. Before he left, he promised that he would sue me.

I'm not sure who reported this incident to internal affairs, but I received a call a few days later. I was advised to come into the internal affairs office. I was advised that a complaint had been lodged against me. I was read my Garrety rights and asked if I wanted a "union rep." Well, yeah, now that you asked. Anytime someone asks you if you want your union representative, the answer should be yes. A union representative was called, and I was interviewed. As I went over the story, I had to explain what I was thinking at the time of the incident. I had to explain why I didn't ask for more information on the description of the person. There was not enough time. I had to explain how I made it there so quickly. I had to explain the language I used or didn't use. I was the bad guy now, or at least it felt that way.

After the interview, I was released. There was not much information on what was going to happen now. Later, I was advised the tapes from the dispatch had been pulled. The internal affairs officers basically listened to them to see what information they could gather from the dispatch to see if my report matched my actions. While they advised there might have been some things I could have done differently, they concluded that I had done the right thing. They concluded that most officers in my situation what have taken the same actions. Most importantly, they concluded that I did not violate the male's rights or the law.

Is this the end of the story? Not even close. Approximately a year later, I was contacted by the male's lawyer, who advised that he was suing me for false arrest, defamation of character and injuries that he had received as a result of the arrest. The male advised that he received, and was still suffering from, back injuries from when I slammed him on the ground during the arrest. I recalled the incident immediately but not in the manner you would expect. For the male, apparently, it was a horrific day, but of course for me, I think it was a Wednesday. I was advised that I was being sued for 75,000 dollars for my actions. I was told the department was being sued as well. This was the first time I had been sued. I was quite afraid. I didn't have 75,000 dollars. Hell, I didn't have 7500 dollars. After I was notified of the lawsuit, it was a few weeks before I had my meeting with the lawyer. I was under the impression the entire time that, if I lost, I would be homeless. I thought about quitting this job because I felt I hadn't done anything wrong. I felt that if I hadn't done anything wrong, then if the occasion called for it, I would take the same action again and as a byproduct, eventually be in the same situation.

After a year of back and forth between the department and many depositions, the department decided they would settle. I was thinking, *Settle! We should discuss this first.* Now, imagine for a moment that you were told you had done everything right, but somehow you still were in this situation. I was thinking maybe the department had to pay a portion and I had to pay a portion. I was thinking maybe the department would pay my share. Maybe they would let me pay in installments.

Two years and some change, this was about how long this whole debacle had lasted. I was getting sick because I was thinking of how I could hide my already meager assets from lawyers and the like. The department's lawyer eventually advised me that because the department had done an internal investigation and had found my actions appropriate, my personal assets were safe.

This was the relief that I needed. To be honest, I no longer cared what happened in these proceedings. I didn't want to go to any more depositions or be polite to this lawyer who seemed to insult me at every turn, the lawyer who went over my internal affairs record and found nothing. The male's lawyer had been speaking to people in the neighborhood where I had been policing for the last two years. He had been knocking on people's doors in an effort to dig up dirt. He had been trying to find someone who I had treated unfairly. He was trying to find someone with a similar complaint to say that I treat people badly. Fortunately, the strangest thing happened. He could find no one. He had spoken to all the witnesses that had been outside watching the entire event. There were plenty of people who witnessed this event. He still found no one who said I acted rashly. I could not have been prouder.

But why? Why would the department settle with the man if I had done everything right? The thing that kept coming up was, "You have the right to resist an unlawful arrest." I understood this. However, I was not set up or trained to deal with a situation like this. Simply because this person had a particular bias against the police, he made the situation evolve the way it did. I was motivated by the fact that someone was possibly hurt and needed my assistance. I am not a good Samaritan. This is my actual job. I didn't feel I had time to mend the relationship between the department and this person at that time.

The department eventually settled with this male for thousands of dollars, not as many thousands as he wanted but still more than I had lying around. Unfortunately for him, he had been going to the chiropractor for over a year to bolster his claim of injuries. With the doctor and lawyer fees paid, I doubt if he cleared anything. I often trade this story with other officers who have been sued. They always say, "If you haven't been sued, then you ain't doing your job." Now, I'm kind of scared to do my job.

9

Death by Rail/What I Didn't Do

As you have learned, officers get sued. When they take actions that, in someone's opinion, exceed their authority, they get sued. That is not the only hazard officer's face. They are not the only ones to be sued either. Sometimes, what you don't do can hang around for years and haunt you.

The smallest detail can sink the whole case. There are scenarios where the smallest detail, that can seem as self-explanatory as they come, needs to be explained in detail. No matter what the scenario, anything can come back to bite you. When an officer asks you a thousand and one questions that seem redundant to you, there is usually a very good reason. He has to try to anticipate any question that may come. He has to be prepared to explain the simplest thing years, perhaps even a decade later.

At the time, my division was shorthanded. Truth be told, my division is always shorthanded. There is a constant tug of war about which division will handle what situation. The homicide division handles a situation when a person dies or is likely to die. The major assaults division (my division) handles a situation if the person is wounded but is not likely to die. How do we know if someone will die from his or her wounds? You can't ask the medical professionals because they will not say. I think it's some kind of legal issue. I have people who have been shot in the head and lungs, who have survived. I've had people who were shot in the leg; they were up talking to me in good spirits. I come back the next day to find they have died from their injury. My point is, we must handle every case like it's a high-profile homicide.

Late one night, around 11:30 pm or later, I received a call out. I was told there were three people injured, possibly as the result of a fight. Upon my arrival, I was advised three people had fallen off a second-floor balcony, and one person was seriously injured. Upon my arrival, EMS was picking the worst-off victim up off the concrete, and he was being transported to the hospital. All that was left was a blood spot on the ground. The rail of the balcony was on the ground in multiple pieces. It would be easy to say that a person or people had fallen from the balcony, but if that were all that happened, I wouldn't have been called.

I scanned the area as I usually do to see if there were any cameras that might make my job a little easier. There were none. The area was poorly lit. Uniformed patrol officers are supposed to have gathered everyone who was involved in the situation and placed them into separate vehicles so their stories wouldn't be tainted. Perhaps due to the number of people on scene, uniformed officers were unable to ascertain who was involved and who was a bystander. They had one person separated in the back of a marked unit, but everyone else was in a group. Of course, as a result, the story of the incident was convoluted.

Just to give an idea of the scene, the apartment was upstairs and midway on a balcony walkway. There was only one way to get up to the second floor, the steps at the end of the balcony. The walkway between the rail and the apartment doors was about three and a half feet wide. There was barely enough space for two people to pass each other comfortably.

I questioned everyone as I always do. I found that everyone, as usual, tried to distance themselves from any wrongdoing, perceived or otherwise. There was a party in the apartment complex. The party was upstairs in a small apartment. The people invited to the party were all family. Upon speaking to the other people at the party, I found there was an argument that happened prior to people falling over the rail. I soon confirmed three people had actually fallen through the rail and that two were transported to the hospital. They had fallen at the same time. One person landed almost directly on his head. The other two people landed on their feet. Of those two people, one was basically uninjured while one hurt their ankles during the landing. All of the participants of the party were intoxicated, some more than others. One person, a lady, leaned on the rail. As the rail began to give way, she grabbed for the nearest person. Of course, that person, in turn, grabbed the person nearest to them. They all fell two stories. The drunkest person, of course, could not mitigate his fall as a sober person would. He received serious injuries. When he fell, he hit his head on the concrete. While he was conscience, he was not coherent.

After speaking with all of the people on scene, I was pretty sure that an argument had occurred inside of the residence, causing a window to have been broken from the inside. A closer inspection confirmed the broken glass pieces were on the outside. The person who was drunk had stumbled into the glass, breaking it. He had been put out of the residence as a result of his rowdiness. The story all fit together to my satisfaction, not to mention, everyone here was family.

As I checked the scene or, more precisely, I checked the railing. I found the railing was so badly rotten that I could break off a piece in my hand and crumble it up. I advised crime scene to take good pictures of the wood because I was certain this was the cause of the accident. Hindsight says I should have taken a sample of the wood. I didn't, and I can't change that, but I really wish I had.

After clearing the scene, I went to the hospital to speak with the victim who only hurt her ankle. The victim told me that she had leaned on the rail and the rail gave way. The victim told me that as the rail gave way, she reached out. The victim told me her boyfriend grabbed her. She advised that he fell over as well. I assume that all the victims fell as a result. The female and her boyfriend had not been drinking to the extent of the drunken individual. They were able to break their falls with less damage but still serious injuries. The stories were just as I had heard on scene.

Unfortunately, I was never able to speak with the victim who was injured the worst. After a few weeks in a coma, he died. I determined the case was not a homicide. I labeled it an accident and moved on to other cases.

Over a year later, I started receiving subpoenas for a deposition. The date of the deposition was pushed back repeatedly. Basically, they wanted to know why I didn't charge someone with murder. They developed an entire scenario, a plausible scenario mind you, about how the argument led to someone being pushed off the balcony. Of course, they went well into detail about how I did not graduate from an engineering school. I did not have the expertise to say the structure was not sound. I had to prove my case and that I was not negligent in my investigation. But amazingly, during the five-hour deposition about an incident that happened nearly three years prior, do you know what we spent the most time on? I spent at least two hours explaining why I thought the wood was rotten. How was I able to determine the wood was rotten? Could I prove the wood was rotten? I had taken a lot of pictures to demonstrate the wood was rotten, but I did not take a sample. A small piece of the wood would have probably saved a lot of strife. It would have definitely saved me years of depositions. This case kept rearing its ugly head for about five years after the actual incident. The end result was the apartment complex was sued, and the victim's family won. The most important thing I did, in this case, was far less important than what I didn't do.

10

Didn't Steal the Money/What I'm Made Of

Police get accused of stealing money. I can't say how many times I have heard stories of police stealing money. Most times, I take it with a grain of salt because of the source. How can I take a drug dealer's word about the integrity of the person who locked him up? Imagine, in my eyes, someone who would prey on the weakest in society simply to benefit themselves. However, I can't just dismiss the idea out of hand. I simply think that police have too many opportunities to steal if they wanted too. There are too many scenarios that come to mind or that I've been through. I've had a large amount of money in my possession that no one else knew about. I know what stuff I am made of, but I can't speak for others.

The reason I know what I'm made of is not simply because I have morals. I have been tested. People think the test has to be huge; it doesn't. I've had access to nearly thirty thousand dollars that no one else knew about. I've had drug dealers offer five, ten thousand dollars to simply cut them loose on scene. I'm no fool, though. The internal affairs division has been known to place agents in certain situations for investigatory purposes. They will place someone on the street or follow a case from start to finish. They will watch the case, know how much a certain person has on their person and simply follow the case to see if the money is placed into evidence. Every officer knows this is a possibility. I also know that criminals are, you know…criminals. They can't be trusted.

Do you know how much criminals hate police? I do. But do you know they tend to hate certain individual police even more? Criminals carry grudges, whereas police tend not to. Why aren't criminals following police home? It's just my opinion, but I think deep down, the criminals know the police are just doing their jobs. However, let me assure you that when they find out you are a criminal too, that changes everything. That's when you get that Vic Mackey *Shield* action. Criminals don't take issue with taking corrective action on other criminals.

A little backstory is probably needed. In my city, the only prison available for police use is Parish Prison. Parish Prison is almost always full. Imagine that, the prison's full. It's unreasonable to think you can run a city when you have nowhere to place prisoners. A compromise was reached. Parish Prison became a place for those who committed felonies. Those who committed misdemeanors would get a summons and were simply released on scene. This policy presented a problem when it came to those who were the problem. People who get into it with their spouses were a factor. Basically, anyone having disputes who live together could be a problem. If you strike your partner, push him or her, it's just a misdemeanor. The problem comes in when we leave. Are they going to behave? It has happened in the past where, the police leave, the fighting starts again and someone dies. It has happened before, and I'm sure it will happen again. What people don't know is departments get sued because of it, not to mention someone dies.

For all intents and purposes, the summons is an arrest. It's a paper that says you promise to show up to court in reference to this matter.

Once upon a time, we had a "four-hour hold" policy. The policy was one of my favorites. It was a policy that allowed police to hold a suspect in a holding cell for four hours then release them back out into the world. It was especially useful when you had someone who was intoxicated in public. Police have a responsibility to an intoxicated person once they are arrested. If I issue you a summons that says you are too intoxicated to be out on the streets, that's me assuming responsibility. If I then let you go back out into the streets and you get smashed by a car after walking into traffic, there will be a public outcry. "Why didn't the police do something if they knew he was too drunk?" There could then be a valid argument that it's the officer's fault. Parish Prison is not in the business of babysitting people because they are intoxicated. Placing them in the holding cell for four hours was a perfect compromise. They sat in the cell and usually slept the alcohol off. Then, they would be released, no harm, no foul. Remember the Andy Griffith Show? "Ol Otis" always had a spot to rest and sleep off his liquor. It was funny in the show, but it was actually very necessary.

I had a small test. Often, size is just a perspective, so it was big to me. I had a call that showed an individual was intoxicated at a store. This was the local wino. Don't act like you don't know what a wino is. This gentleman routinely begged for money at the store to buy beers and other liquors. I recognized him from the many times I issued him summonses for having an open container. I issued him a bunch, but I knew nothing would happen because he was homeless. My city didn't arrest people for misdemeanor warrants because of the lack of space in Parish Prison. Unfortunately, this gentleman was intoxicated. He was tore down drunk. I couldn't leave him to his own devices. I took him into custody. I placed cuffs on him and searched him. He was extremely dirty and smelled, as it appeared he should be. He had clearly urinated on himself. It was not a pleasure to search him. The job had to be done since he was going into my unit. He had to be transported to the district for a four-hour hold. Upon the search of this gentleman, I found a few items: a lighter, a bottle cap, a small knife and 300-some-odd dollars. I placed the items in my vehicle's cup holder. I transported this smelly individual to the district. He was placed in the cell to sleep it off safely. I continued my patrol. Four hours came and went. I went to the district, picked up the gentleman and took him back to where I picked him up. Truth be told, I think he was still a bit drunk but no longer belligerent. He staggered along his way. A day or two passed and I realized I had not given this gentleman his money. I had seen him multiple times since this incident occurred. He had not waived me down. He had not said anything to me at all.

Clearly, he had been so drunk that he did not remember the arrest. He did not remember the money. I had it. No one else knew about it, and it was only three hundred bucks. I knew this guy was only going to buy alcohol, or at least, I assumed in the depths of my arrogance and ignorance, that he was only going to buy alcohol. I thought about it for what seemed like an hour but was likely only a moment.

It was not my money. This guy probably got social security. This was likely the only money he would have for the month. It was irrelevant what he did with it. I brought this gentleman back his money. He thought he lost it. He thanked me and promptly walked into the liquor store.

This may seem like a small thing, but for me, it meant everything. It let me know what I was made of. I have never been truly tempted on any other occasion.

11

Don't Help Friends Help Yourself

Police tend not to do favors for friends. It's not so much a policy as a good personal guiding principle. If you know a person, then you should avoid the case. Of course, that is if you know a person and it's a friend, and you want to remain friends, you should avoid the case. Officers have found on many occasions that a favor of any magnitude for a friend should be avoided. Don't try to help out your friends. Don't do security for their parties. Don't do any favor that may, in any way, come into conflict with your job. Believe it or not, the friend will not be grateful. Your friend will not be thankful that he has a friend who is a police officer. Your friend will ask for another favor. The thing with favors is, when requested, the goal by the requester is to make them appear as harmless and inconsequential as possible.

Sometime after I was a professional, four years or better, I had a case that I remember quite well. I'm from Dalton Estates. I spent a large part of my teen years there. As a result, I'm well known in the area. I had my own personal circle of friends. My friends knew me well. I still communicated with some of them. When they saw me, I stopped and chatted. Some of them regarded me as a sellout—or worse. Others simply saw me as "J." Well, there was a generation younger than mine. The younger siblings of my friends, I knew them, not as well as I knew my friends, but

I knew them as the little brothers and sisters. Of course, I resigned to look out for them as best I could.

There was one situation involving a kid, or rather a man, who has since been killed. We shall call him Timothy Moon. Timothy was the younger brother of a friend of mine. Timothy was a troublemaker. I told him numerous times, he had to clean up his act. I had never caught him, but I was pretty certain he sold marijuana and perhaps other items. He had a particular hangout spot in front of a set of apartments. One day, I was contacted by the apartment manager, who advised me he wanted the guy to stop hanging out in front of the complex. I stopped and told Timothy to move away from the complex. He did that day. He wound up back in front of the complex about a week later.

The next time, I gathered a bunch of officers together, and we closed in on the location from all directions. We searched the area and found a potato chip bag filled with smaller baggies of marijuana. The potato chip bag was found approximately twenty yards away from the group of people we swarmed. One of those people was Timothy. I was pretty certain that Timothy was the actual seller of the contraband, but I did not find it on his person, and I did not charge the entire group like had been done in the past. However, I did run everyone's name. It turned out that Timothy had warrants, traffic mostly. Whether fortunate or not, it was a misdemeanor warrant. Timothy was not booked into prison because Parish Prison was filled, and there was no room for misdemeanor prisoners. I simply advised Timothy of his warrants and released him.

Fast forward to a few months later. I received a call that said a victim was at the hospital suffering from a gunshot wound to the leg. Upon speaking to the victim, we asked the simple question, "Do you know who shot you?" He promptly responded, "Timothy Moon. He shot me because he said I stole his drugs."

Well, it was established that Timothy shot the victim. It was established that Timothy had a gun. That would make for a dangerous situation when the police go to approach him. When the police do approach him, any movement could cause him to be killed. I didn't want that to happen. Being that he was the brother of a friend, I decided that I would contact him and take him into custody. This, at least in my mind, is a favor, not only to Timothy but also to his brother, who was my friend.

I knew just where to go to locate Timothy. I took a couple units and had them give me a wide birth. I approached Timothy, as I always had, and took him into custody without incident. This was a favor. Upon searching Timothy, I found no drugs or anything illegal. However, I did find a large amount of money in his pocket. Most often, any money found on your person would be booked into evidence or, at the very least, placed into his personal property. This would have the money out of use for the time he was in prison. In most cases, you get girlfriends calling about the money saying things like that was the light bill money, or that was the money for school clothes. Whatever the case, I allowed Timothy to give the money to his brother before taking him into custody. This was a favor.

Timothy was charged with, or rather, I charged Timothy with, second-degree aggravated battery with a firearm. This was a favor. Timothy was extremely upset, not because he had been charged for shooting the victim. He was upset because he was charged with second-degree aggravated battery with a firearm. He was upset about the firearm caveat. How was I supposed to charge this fool without adding the firearm? He shot someone. He could have been charged with attempted murder. He could have possibly been charged with attempted first-degree murder because there were drugs involved. While I was booking Timothy, we were at the district. Timothy began to call out everything he knew about me. He mentioned who my family was, basically to establish that he knew me on a personal level, after which, of course, he waited until he had gotten the attention of my lieutenant to start making comments such as, "Hey, you gonna do this to me? We smoked weed together." I actually thought it was pretty smart in the manner in which he had done it. I just didn't think that after all the favors I had done for him that he would take that route.

Of course, I had never partaken of the "sticky icky" with this idiot. I'd never hung out with this person on any occasion. We had never sat down and shot the breeze. I was a friend of his older brother. That was the entirety of our relationship. Needless to say, I was "randomly" chosen for five random drug tests that year alone. Previous to that statement, I had been chosen for said random test once over the span of four years.

Most drug dealers eventually end up dead or in jail. Timothy was a drug dealer and a short while later, went the way of most drug dealers. Rest in peace, Timothy.

12

Seriously Though, Help Yourself First.

As I have previously stated, I'm from Dalton Estates. I know a lot of people there. Due to a four-year stint in the military, I hadn't lived there in a few years. Of course, people change. Being a low-income area, Dalton Estates changed its population at a more rapid pace. After Hurricane Katrina, Dalton Estate filled up rapidly. Due to its low-cost apartments, it was filled to capacity. Unfortunately, when New Orleans went underwater, the majority of the people who were hurt were poor people. As well-adjusted people, we arrogantly assume poor people are just lazy. It turns out a lot of the poor people had mental problems and other issues. This left Dalton Estates a ripe area for people who had mental issues and disabilities. Of course, there was no vetting process, and the absentee landlords adopted a philosophy of "the more, the merrier."

I tend to want to help people. It's a good trait to have for a police officer. A good friend of mine has a nephew. The nephew was about fourteen years old at the time of these events. He had lived in the area his whole life. The kid had a unique look to him. Dalton Estates was majority black people. There were a few white people in the area, and the storeowners were Asian and Middle Eastern. At the time, there was a shortage of Hispanic people. That has since changed quite a bit, but that's another story. The nephew was a mixed kid. His mother was black, and his father was white. Oddly enough, the nephew looked Mexican.

When all the new people started showing up in Dalton Estates, they were not welcomed immediately. There were a lot of people who did not like them. The new groups of people came in droves. They filled the apartments, outnumbering the previous tenants. There were fights and new burglaries in the area. The morale of the neighborhood took a nosedive. The basketball courts, playgrounds, and game rooms were crowded along with every other recreational area. There were always people hanging out on the corners, and even worse, people hanging around outside, making noise all night. The neighborhood was getting worse. If I'm being honest, it was never a great place, to begin with. There was always crime as there always is any time you have a surplus of poor people. However, there are unspoken rules in every neighborhood. There are people who you don't bother.

For example, Mrs. Latrice is never to be bothered. Why is Mrs. Latrice never to be bothered? Mrs. Latrice is one of the nicest people you will ever meet. She has fed all of the children in the neighborhood for years. When there is a family in need, she always helps them out. She is an avid churchgoer. Her son was killed when he was ten years old, and as a result, she has basically adopted every child in the neighborhood. I don't mean figuratively; she was a foster mother to at least ten little boys over a twenty-year span. The majority of those boys did well for themselves. This was before my time. I know this because I lived in the neighborhood. I knew she was a nice lady. I'm not a bad guy, so I would never dream of doing her any harm. However, I noticed that she would walk to the store at night without a care in the world. I would walk her there and back if I saw her, just to be certain she was safe. She would talk all about her time in the neighborhood. I could see that the older people respected her. If older people respected her, the children coming up were inclined to respect her as well. The "children" who were now grown also made sure their children knew to respect her. This would be common knowledge for everyone, at least for everyone from the neighborhood. New people wouldn't know that. For most people, that wouldn't matter because a nice old lady would never be a target. However, a criminal is a criminal is a criminal. When Mrs. Latrice was robbed on her way to the store, all hell broke loose.

As she usually does, Mrs. Latrice walked to the corner store for whatever she needed on that particular night. It was not especially late, perhaps just past sunset. After leaving the store, someone stopped Mrs. Latrice and asked her for a dollar. When Mrs. Latrice got her wallet out to give the dollar to the unnamed male, he grabbed the wallet out of her hand. Mrs. Latrice was so shocked by the incident she attempted to hold on to it. She fell to the ground as a result of the tug from the unnamed male.

Mrs. Latrice was not injured as a result of this incident. The police were quick to act on this case. The culprit was arrested within about two hours. It was a new person in the neighborhood, a person who didn't know who Mrs. Latrice was. Everyone else knew who Mrs. Latrice was.

Shortly after that, there began a series of attacks. Every couple of days, there would be a report of someone, always a newcomer, having been attacked. They would be sent to the hospital with mostly minor lacerations and contusions. When the newcomers were questioned, they would say a group of teenagers had attacked them. They would give various descriptions of suspects. One description of a suspect that was constantly given was a young "Mexican boy."

While this was not "open and shut," it was clear the suspect was the nephew. The next step was to put the nephew in a photographic lineup. We showed the victim the picture and saw if he or she identified him. Would you believe it? They didn't identify him. Perhaps I was wrong on my assumption. Maybe there was another teenage Mexican kid in the area. I started to think that maybe I had misjudged the nephew.

I was just about certain I had made a mistake until a call was received in reference to a disturbance. When we arrived, I found the nephew was a part of a large group of juveniles who were about to fight another group of juveniles. One group was an assortment of long-time Dalton Estates residents. The other group was all newcomers. There were about thirty people involved. Among that sea of people, there appeared to be only one Mexican kid.

I was again certain the nephew was my suspect. In the words of the illustrious Alonzo from *Training Day*, "It's not what you know. It's what you can prove." The victims would not cooperate. They would not identify the nephew as the suspect. Fine. I hold no grudges.

The nephew was the nephew of a friend of mine. I spoke to that friend and told him the details of the situation. I was not surprised that he was not surprised. While he did not openly say he knew his nephew was involved, he did give me that impression. I told him to speak with his nephew to end this campaign before someone got seriously hurt or something happened purposely, or incidentally that couldn't be undone. My friend told me his nephew was incorrigible and that he would be wasting his breath. He told me I was welcome to try to speak with him myself. I figured it was worth a shot.

Upon speaking to the nephew, I told him I knew he was one of the persons committing these batteries. I told him there would likely be no charges, as there was not enough evidence to move forward with…yet. I told him if these batteries ended now, it was likely this would be the last he would hear of it. I did not ask him any questions, which would violate his rights. I did not allow him to speak on the matter; I simply made the statement so he could understand.

I spoke with the kid off and on after that—nothing too in-depth. "How is school going? Have you filled out any applications?" I told him about when I was a kid, I cut grass as a hustle. I told him how I had a couple people working for me. My point was to keep the kid out of trouble by making him aware someone cared and was watching.

Though I was not the officer called out, I started hearing about more batteries being committed against newcomers by a group of juveniles. The nephew started "hitting corners" when he saw my unit approach. My conscience was clear. I had done my due diligence as a police officer and a friend. I had done more than his uncle or his parents. I resigned myself to stop the violence in my neighborhood.

Eventually, one of the victims of the group of youths was tired of getting jumped. By this time, I had gathered all the friends and associates of the nephew. It didn't take a genius to realize his friends were the other suspects. Finally, I had a victim who iden-tified the persons who attacked him. Nine people were arrested as a result of this one victim stepping up—simple battery, a misde-meanor charge, but a clear path to deter any future batteries. If another occurred, we would know just who our suspects were. Case closed…you would think.

Time goes on at its designated pace regardless of what we do to slow or rush it. I eventually made detective and moved off the streets. The nephew continued his endeavors. His endeavors con-flicted with my endeavors, so we eventually met again.

The nephew was a rotten egg. The thing about rotten eggs is you don't know they are rotten until its lunchtime. The nephew got progressively worse. He was getting involved in more and more altercations. I spoke with his mother, who advised me in no uncertain terms that I was mistaken.

I got a call that stated a mentally disabled person had been battered. These are the kinds of cases I handle; no big deal. This was one of a hundred other cases I had. It didn't stand out, initially. When I contacted this man to interview him about his case, he told me his story. He told me that he and his wife were from New Orleans. He advised they both received social security due to their "mental deficiencies." He received a check of 600 dollars a month, and his wife received about the same. The man worked odd jobs in the area to make ends meet.

The man advised that a local young thug had started asking him for money. He said, at first, he gave him twenty dollars. The man said the thug returned and became ever more violent. The man advised that the thug eventually was taking his entire check. The thug would wait at the corner store on the day the man cashed his check. He would then take the man's money. While this went on for a while, the man decided he would go to another place to cash his check. This would avoid the entire situation. The man advised that later in the day, he heard a knock on the door. When he went to answer the door, the thug pushed it open. He beat the man up in front of his wife and took the money. Neighbors called the police when they heard the racket.

The man was well-liked in the area. In the apartment complex where the man lived, he functioned as a handyman. He painted, picked up trash and was generally a nice man.

The neighbors were really upset about the incident. I questioned all of the people in the apartment complex. As usual, no one really had any information to present. As usual, I passed out my card to everyone with whom I'd come into contact. This was not unusual; people don't want to get involved. This case was not usual, and I received calls, a lot of calls. It seemed people were really upset about the incident. I identified the nephew as the thug in no time.

A warrant was issued for the arrest of the nephew. He was located on a street near the man's residence. He was arrested by uniformed patrol officers, and I was summoned to the scene. Upon speaking with the nephew, I read him his rights per Miranda as I normally would. By this time, the nephew was seventeen years of age. In Louisiana, this age is considered a legal adult, at least at this time. The nephew's mother arrived very soon and became irate, as mothers do. She was upset because she was certain her son could not be the culprit. Furthermore, she was certain that I was only arresting her son because of a grudge I had been holding against her son. At this moment, the officer on scene pointed out the nephew had over 400 dollars on his person. However, the nephew did not have a job.

The nephew was transported to my office to be interviewed. I allowed his mother to come to the office as a courtesy. His story was ridiculous, to say the least. He stated the man gave him the money out of the kindness of his heart. The mother was allowed to come to the office out of the kindness of my heart when we interviewed her son. However, she was not allowed to be present during the interview. When she was advised of the story the nephew had given, she became extremely irate and had to be escorted out of the building. The nephew was booked into Parish Prison.

Almost immediately after his arrest (a few days), I was forwarded an email from my lieutenant advising I had a complaint in internal affairs. This was not my first.

The mother had written a letter to the chief of police. The mother said that police (me) had arrested her son on a false charge of armed robbery (not quite the right charge but close enough). The mother said she spoke with the victim who advised he was not even going to show up to court. Side note "witness intimidation" is when the suspect or an affiliate of the suspect communicates with the victim and conveys a threat or causes the victim to feel that there will be negative consequences to following up with the case and witness intimidation is a crime. The mother said she knew police had the right to stop her son. She also knew he had rights too. The mother said, in her letter, that the officer in question (me) had taken her son and driven him around the neighborhood in the back of a police car as if he was some kind of informant. While I'll admit that's not beneath me, it was a false accusation. However, one of the lieutenants or captains in the email chain actually said he thought he remembered this complaint, thereby adding validity to this baseless accusation. The mother made the statement that, if I were not taken care of, she would go to the "media."

The complaint had already made the rounds starting from the chief and finally filtered down to me. I knew this was the case because the email had simply been forwarded. The history of the original letter was still there. I could see all the different stops the letter had made and the responses of the officers to whom it was addressed.

The comments ranged from, "What is this officer doing?" to "Sounds like good police work to me." Officers were asking if I had a personal grudge against the nephew. It wasn't long before it was discovered that I was friends with his uncle. The mother let that information fly almost immediately.

The case was brought forth to be investigated, not the details of the case, which I so meticulously documented, not all of the details that I placed in report after report, not the witness statements, not the facts of the case. No! What was investigated was the relationship that I'd had with the family and any slight I may have received from the nephew that might cause me to carry a grudge.

The nephew was no saint. He'd had plenty of run-ins with the law that had nothing to do with me. He continued his descent into being a full-blown criminal without my help. The internal affairs investigation was not sustained. That means they didn't think it was a valid case (the one against me).

Between the nephew's trial date and the incident, he'd had other incidents as well. In one of those incidents, he shot at his mother, yep, the letter writer. This action further cemented the decision of internal affairs to make the case against me unsubstantiated.

The victim did indeed show up to court. He testified as well. The nephew received five years.

In hindsight, what did I do wrong? I made it personal. I tried to redeem this kid instead of taking action. Perhaps I should even have taken this case to another officer to follow up on, once I realized the relationship. My personal involvement with this case could have allowed the nephew to go free. He would not have paid for his crimes and would have likely continued to escalate his actions. One could easily reason the mother would have taken this action with any officer who arrested her son. The personal relationship gave the claim weight that it would not otherwise have had.

Since this case, I haven't heard anything else about the nephew. I also haven't kept in contact with my friend.

13

The Enemy is Thy Self/That Includes Family

Officers learn that favors are not good. There are rules that supersede profession. If you have siblings, those bonds are important. Family is no exception.

As a rule, officers tend to avoid any family issues. You cannot be a police officer and an uncle, aunt or cousin. There will be, I repeat, there will be a conflict of interest. Everyone wants to be the hero, even if it's a police officer. We want to be the hero too, especially to our family. Any veteran officer will tell you that being a hero to your family is irrelevant. The smallest and most insignificant argument among family can turn into the worst scenario for a police officer.

After about three years working on the job, I had this law enforcement thing licked. I knew how to handle myself. I received a call from my younger sister telling me that her boyfriend and his family were at her house arguing with her. She told me they wanted her boyfriend's father to live with them. He was disabled. My sister simply didn't want that responsibility. I could more than understand that. As bad as it may seem, I wouldn't want that responsibility myself. In my mind, I was going to be the person I always was, the strong, calm (devilishly handsome) mediator.

When I got there, there was a huge argument going on in the front yard. My sister had called my aunts who had come to defend her. Her boyfriend and his mother and sister were there, and there was just a thunderous ruckus. When I got there, I told everyone to calm down. I told the boyfriend's people and mine to leave. I said this was an argument between the boyfriend and his girl-friend. I told my people to leave. My people were inclined to leave because I had told them, and I carried some weight with that clan. However, they refused to leave until the boyfriend's people left.

On the other hand, the boyfriend's people couldn't care less about my opinion. I told them they needed to leave or my sister would call the police. I told them that if the police came, they would charge them with entry and remaining after being forbid-den. I told them this was not worth getting charged. My sister lived outside of the city limits, so even if she had called the police, they would come from a different agency. They refused to leave. I had my sister call the police. I stood to the side until the police arrived. When the police arrived, I explained the situation—not my side or their sides, more along the position of there were no weapons on scene. I stayed until the officer declared the scene safe. I then left the scene.

Before I made it back to my office (about a fifteen-minute drive), my sergeant had gotten calls from the boyfriend's family saying that I had threatened to arrest them all. Apparently, I was throwing my weight around and was yelling and cursing everyone. At the time, there were no body cameras or recorders. Even if I did have a camera, I likely would not have activated it because I considered this a personal matter and not work.

Regardless of my intentions, if I had not had my history working for me, I may have been in some serious trouble. The officer from the other agency who handled the case spoke to my supervisor about what he had witnessed and what the people on the scene had told him happened. Of course, they didn't tell him I had threatened them in any way because, at the time, they hadn't thought of the story. I did not get into trouble…that day.

Weeks later, yes, weeks later, my sister married the boyfriend. A short time after that, less than a year, I invited my sister to my house for a function, and she brought his family. It took everything in me not to lose it. She had brought the enemy to my house and had not even thought twice about it. It occurred to me that she did not see them as the enemy even though it appeared that way that day. It will never work out for anyone involving themselves in someone else's relationship matters. Anyone in a relationship will tell you that a fight is only temporary. If the fight has not become violent, stay out of it. This goes doubly so for a police officer.

As a more mature officer, I now understand that my mere presence was an intimidation factor that my sister may or may not have been aware of when she called me. The boyfriend's people were very aware of it. Even though I can truly say that I intended to be a big brother that day, I came as an officer. I had no business involving my police department in an altercation outside of its jurisdiction. If the situation had become violent, I would have been forced to react. If I had reacted, how would my decision-making skills cope with the fact that my family was on scene? It likely would have been extremely biased. It would likely cause injury to someone who didn't need to be injured, opening the department and myself to litigation—even worse, opening myself to criminal charges.

My sister did not try to hurt me. She bore me no ill will. However, she was doing like most people do. She was looking out for herself. This was not an act of narcissism, but more likely, negligence. She did not think about how the situation would affect my job or my life. As an officer, I have to think about the entire situation. Every time I take action, I am taking action on behalf of my entire organization. Even when the action doesn't seem to involve anything public, the action is an organizational move. The decision is rarely yours alone.

14

The Reason We/I Don't Allow the Use of the Cellphone

During traffic stop situations, the officer usually starts off dealing with an angry person. No one wants a ticket. Aside from the inherent conflict, the next point of conflict starts with the phone, specifically, when the officer tells the person to put that phone down. You've seen it over and over. The officer is trying to gather information while the driver has the phone in his face, recording. Even worse, the officer is trying to get information while you are talking on the phone.

As a police officer, we have to establish control over the scene. As an officer, I do not want to separate you from the world. I more than realize the phone is your connection to the world. I can understand that people want to record the conversation, whether video or audio. I don't care. Record whatever you need to. However, keep in mind that I have a mission that I need to accomplish. I need to do it in the most time-efficient and safest means possible. I know you have a life you are living and I want you to get back to it as soon as possible. I need you to put your phone down and give me your full attention.

I think one of the largest misconceptions out there is that when a police officer is on a stop, you are in danger. The truth is, the whole time the officer is on scene with you, he is exposed. He wants to finish up with you as soon as possible so he can get back to safety. You know who the officer is. He has his name on his shirt. He has where he works written on his shirt and car. On the other hand, they know nothing about you. Are you a killer just leaving your last victim or just someone's grandmother? It's a surprise. We only find out after we are standing next to you. By then, if you're the first one, it's likely too late for the officer.

From the point of view of the citizen given from the point of view of my sisters and family members, you want to make sure you document the stop. That is awesome, and I support that action, but…put your phone down and cooperate with me. Give me the items I need. Give me your attention. You documenting the incident, that's your assignment, your priority. If you can accomplish your mission without hindering mine, that would be great.

When my wife, sister or female relative is pulled over, I tell them, if you feel you need to call someone, do it when you first see the lights. Tell the person where you are and put the phone down. As long as the phone is not hindering your cooperation, the officer won't be bothered by it. Get the items out that you know the officer will ask for (license, registration and insurance). Have the items ready when the officer arrives at the car. Best-case scenario, you have everything in order, and he gives you a warning. Worst-case scenario, you get a ticket. Of course, this is if you are a law-abiding citizen, no warrants, or extras.

I was lucky or unlucky enough, depending on the point of view, to work in an area where my mother lived. I would visit from time to time while on duty to eat or make use of the facilities. I made it a point not to cause any problems in the area where my mother lived. By not causing any problems, I mean, I rarely stopped cars or issued tickets in that area. Who would want to put their mother in danger? Police are always concerned that someone they love will be hurt by someone they arrested.

It was a day like any other, I was headed to my mother's house to eat, converse or whatever. Just before I turned the corner where my mother lives, I saw a Chevy Suburban blatantly run a stop sign. She turned right, and her vehicle passed mine. As she passed, I could clearly see the driver was a female. Because we were so close to my mother's house, I was almost inclined not to even stop her, but there were too many people outside, not to mention children playing. I activated my bar lights, made the U-turn and pulled her over. I intended to give her a verbal warning. I wanted her to simply be aware of her surroundings. She stopped, and I approached the vehicle. Upon contacting her, she was already on the phone. I asked her for her license, registration and insurance. "I've stopped you because you've just run a stop sign." The woman ignored me as she talked on the phone. I repeated my order in a slightly more authoritative tone. "Ma'am, I need your license, registration and insurance." The woman again ignored me. I then called the stop in. I advised the woman to put away the phone and follow my orders. After the woman refused to acknowledge my presence, I opened the car door and asked for back up. I could hear her on the phone telling someone she had been stopped by the police and giving her location. I again told her to put the phone away. The woman completely ignored me. I advised the woman of the caveat on all tickets in Louisiana. "Ma'am, this ticket is in lieu of arrest. This is not an admission of guilt. It's just saying you will show up to court. Ma'am, this is your last opportunity to cooperate. I need your license, registration and insurance." She again ignored me. At this point, this simple traffic stop had turned into an arrest situation. I placed my hand around her left arm in an effort to get her out of the vehicle, and she began to resist. By resist, I mean actively pull away.

I will pause for a moment to say, I usually wouldn't have let this go this far. I simply didn't want to arrest her or even give her a ticket for that matter. I just wanted to give her a verbal warning and then be on my way. I guess because of this one-track mind, I ignored the obvious signs that there was more going on than meets the eye. Usually, when someone refuses to cooperate on this level, it's because they have warrants or something along those lines. Once my senses came back into focus, I put away the thoughts of giving her a warning. I now had to identify her. Since she refused to cooperate, that meant she had to be taken into custody. This is where most officers get into trouble. They are doing their job, and a civilian refuses to cooperate. Then, they expect the officer to simply leave or give up or something other than continue the course. As a police officer, though, we really don't have that option. We have to do our job. So, as I struggled to get her out of the car, she has locked onto the steering wheel. I am certain I could have gotten her out of the car if I absolutely had to. The only problem was she was a woman, and I did not want to hurt her…although she deserved it.

The method I used was called pressure points, which are used for those who are passively resisting. As I struggled to get her out of the car and she screamed as if I'm killing her, I saw someone out of the corner of my eye. They pulled up in a car and immediately exited their vehicle. It was a male. He came running up to me full speed. As I have already said, I only saw this person out of the corner of my eye while dealing with an irate female. I could see this was not a police officer. The vehicle was not a unit. The person was not wearing a blue uniform, which is the department standard.

As this person approached me at a full sprint, I was so startled I drew my weapon. I placed it eye level and started squeezing the trigger. My sidearm, a forty-caliber Glock, has an eight-pound trigger squeeze. This means I have to squeeze the trigger with eight pounds of pressure to fire. I would swear I had pulled it to seven pounds. The man apparently did not recognize his situation until his forehead was pressed up against the barrel of my firearm. It was only then that he started to retreat. I saw the face of anger immediately melt away only to be replaced by fear and then understanding. As I had one hand on this female refusing to leave her car and one hand on the trigger of my weapon, which was pointed at the head of this stranger, I realized this was who she was on the phone with. This was her ol' man, her boyfriend, brother or whomever. He had come to rescue her. I didn't know what his intentions were because he approached me so fast. There was a possibility that he would have stopped and said, "Sir, I wish to have a word with you about this matter." He also could have jumped on my back in an effort to kill me. Since I was paying attention to my surroundings, I am thankful to never know. She had been calling him on the phone while I had been standing there. I had allowed this call to continue for far too long. I had called for backup, but hers arrived first.

I was in this awkward position, which I could only hold due to the position I was in. I held the position until backup arrived. Even with ten officers on scene, we still had a hard time getting her out of the vehicle. We had to pepper spray her and pry her hands loose from the steering wheel. She was arrested for running a stop sign and resisting arrest. It turns out she had no insurance. Her vehicle was towed. Her boyfriend nearly died because she didn't have insurance on her vehicle. The boyfriend was a convicted felon. He had been arrested three times in the past for battery on an officer and other assorted crimes. He was not arrested this day because he did not break any laws.

I don't know how serious that was for her. Having your car towed at an inopportune time can make the whole house of cards tumble down. I understand. But let's be clear. What she did was wrong and nearly got someone killed. Now, when I approach a vehicle, the driver must put down the phone and talk to me. I more than understand that in certain situations, women don't feel comfortable out alone with an officer. I have no problem pulling up to a busy gas station or other populated place. But there can be no phone calls made until I have assessed the situation.

15

Extra Duty

Officers work! People see an officer at a detail sitting in his unit, and they think, "He's getting paid for nothing." No one pays anyone for free. Some jobs are easier than others. Allow me to help you understand the officer's job is not an easy one. Even though it appears he is just sitting in the car, there are a lot of factors at play. Any minute, he could be called into a terrifying situation. If you look closely, you will see he is likely backed up in a corner so that he can see everything. Sometimes, he is watching you. Sometimes, he is just trying to be safe. Sometimes, he can barely keep his eyes open because this is his sixteenth hour of work.

The best thing about being a police officer is extra duty. Not all departments, but my department doesn't pay well. It paid decently when I started, but we haven't gotten a raise in ten years. To be honest, I think most police officers are underpaid for what they do. The redeeming factor of the job is the abundant extra duty. An officer can make large sums of money if he is willing to work. Most of the officers I know work a minimum of sixty hours a week. It's a hard life. Trading time for money is always a losing proposition. You will never be able to replace the time. The pay will never be enough. With that philosophical jewel dropped, officers look for the details with minimal effort required. A police officer's job is dangerous. If an officer were to be killed on duty, it's a tragedy. For an officer to be killed doing extra duty, that's a damn shame.

In my off time, I was working as security in an apartment complex that was in my patrol area. I worked evening shift, which was 2:00 pm until 12:00 am. After 12:00 am, I would arrive at this apartment complex and park in a conspicuous spot so that anyone coming there could see my vehicle and perhaps not cause any problems. These details were the ones the rookie officers would love to have, but the senior officers know better. The reason the details are so coveted among the young officers is because of money. These kinds of details require a lot of hours. The hours are usually very flexible. The officer can make his own hours and show up whenever he isn't working. That means there is a lot of money to be made. This is extra duty gold for a young officer.

The senior, more seasoned, officer never wants this detail. He knows what the job actually entails. The apartment complex is always cheap, so they never, ever hire enough officers. The officer knows that he cannot effectively cover the entire complex himself. He knows the complex manager will call him personally whenever there's a problem. He knows they don't care if he is at work or not. He also knows that if anything occurs at the complex, he will be on scene almost immediately and there by himself until help arrives. Also, and I can't stress this enough, senior officers don't want to work. They don't want a detail that's going to be like their day jobs. They don't want to have to arrest someone every day.

I was a rookie when I took this detail. I was so excited because I had seen older, more senior, officers in charge of a detail who had twenty officers working for them. The benefit was first the officer was paid an administrative fee. This means he gets money for writing the schedule (which, for the most part, doesn't change) and other things. In my mind, he gets free money. The department's ranks structure does not matter when it comes to a detail. If I am in charge of the detail and a captain wants a position, then he works for me. When I got the call, it was because I had handled a call in this particular complex. The manager was thinking of getting some security and asked me if I could set it up. I certainly could! The manager advised he had about forty hours a week he wanted covered. I immediately called up my classmates from the academy. I took twenty hours myself because, money. Then, I split the other hours up among three officers. I was in charge, and so I laid down the ground rules and how I wanted this handled. I explained to the officers this could be a lot of money in our pockets if we just did it right.

You would think that having commissioned officers working for you, the detail would basically run itself. I had officers showing up late. I had officers not showing up at all and claiming: "I was in the back. You didn't see me?" When the officers were there, they had work to do. There were constantly people smoking marijuana in empty apartments. People were habitually playing loud music in their cars as they entered the complex. There was just a constant effort on our part to get the place under control. Still worse, while we worked to get the place under control, the landlord was refusing to do his part. The names we gave him were not being evicted per our threats. That means the people we were dealing with had to be dealt with over and over again. Ideally, when we gave the management the names of the problems, the management was to then start the process of evicting these people. Getting rid of them would make the complex a safer and/or more desirable place to live. The huge flaw in this process is the complex was often being sold from one owner to another. When the new owner takes possession of the property, he wants to lay down the law. He hires police to make the place safe and set precedence. However, the new landlord cannot afford to evict all the people causing the problems because they pay rent and the landlord needs that rent. This is where we come to an impasse. The apartment manager is filling the apartment complex with a bunch of problem people because he needs to fill the complex and get paid.

After a while, though, after cutting some officers and adding new ones, we got a good team together. We started to get that coveted reputation of, "Them boys don't play." We got to the point where we would come into the apartment complex for the night, and the whole place would shut down. There was little traffic save for people coming and going for work or whatever their needs were. The constant hanging out disappeared. We had done it. We had set this detail up to be a good one. It would run on autopilot. The people who were still there were happy that we were there. The people who were the problem had moved out on their own because they couldn't do as they pleased. Can you guess what happened next? Yep, we were let go because the complex manager no longer needed us. There was no problem at the complex, so why would they need security? I was fine. I left with no issues. I had made a lot of money, and neither my people nor myself had been hurt. I did feel I had been used. Six months later, we were rehired. Still a young officer, I took the gig. We were let go after about two months this time. I made a lot of money, but I won't do it again.

16

Incidentally, While Working the Complex

Officers never know what's going to happen. We don't know where the day is going to lead. We do our best to be prepared for any scenario. We still get surprised regularly. The surprise is not always bad. Sometimes, a stranger will pay for our meal. Sometimes, someone will come back and say thank you for that thing you did. Sometimes, the surprises are bad.

I was working a complex that was in my area where I patrol daily anyway. I figured I could patrol during the daytime and keep it under control. Unfortunately for me, even when I was patrolling the apartment complex, the complex was large. So, it was always difficult to monitor the entire place. You move to one side; the people causing problems would simply move to the other side of the complex and hang out. It was my job to basically find the people who were the problem, charge them and alert the management.

I had been having an ongoing problem with a young woman who was a tenant at this complex. I had multiple encounters with this tenant for various reasons.

One of these encounters was me standing by at her apartment while the local furniture rental place officials attempted to reclaim their furniture. While the company tried to get the furniture, she advised them her apartment had been broken into. A quick scan of the apartment showed the items, a fifty-two-inch television included, were not in the apartment. Actually, a quick scan showed there was no furniture in the apartment, no couches, chairs, etcetera. The young woman had previously called out the police (other police) to file a report of burglary, and she had the file number on hand.

Later, purely out of curiosity, I looked up the report. I noticed the entry point was the window. I should mention the apartment was upstairs. The window was located next to the front door. The window was small. If I had to estimate, I would say the window's clearing was approximately thirty or so inches. I assumed the burglar went into the apartment through the window and simply exited with the items through the door. However, I did recall there was a double lock on the door, you know, the kind that require a key on both sides. Also, it is necessary to note that there was no damage to the door. I suspected that something was amiss. However, I had enough work on my plate already. I didn't need to add to it by following up on a fake burglary. Better leave that to the detectives. Besides, this was not an uncommon situation. It seems that a lot of burglars burgled places that rented furniture. They did this just before the bill was due.

I had another unrelated encounter with this same female that involved her fighting with the neighbor. She was arrested and booked into prison. It was at this time I found out she was HIV positive. This is not uncommon. I have dealt with plenty of cases involving people suffering from HIV. I would like to say, I treat them no different from any other person. That would be a lie. I am cautious. I am even more cautious than I am with other criminals. I know all about the disease. I know what is required to be infected. I also know when people are under stress, they react in unexpected ways. How much more stress can you be under than to be HIV positive and going to jail? I am especially careful.

While working this awesome detail, I got a disturbance call on the far side of the complex. It appeared that two neighbors were fighting. One of the neighbors had run inside her apartment to escape. The female who had been a constant source of complaints was the aggressor. The victim fled inside of her own residence. The female continued to pursue the other victim. She had taken her fist and punched through the window of the fleeing victim. As a result of the glass breaking, the female had a large gash on her arm. While she was not currently on scene, I was able to follow where she had gone. There was a large trail of blood leading directly back to her upstairs apartment. The trail of blood was so thick that I was pretty certain that she would likely be in the apartment dead or near death. I did not want to go in, as I could see blood on the floor and walls of the apartment from the outside. However, I could not just allow this female to bleed to death. I entered this apartment, which in my cautious state, I noticed was well furnished. This was the same apartment that had been emptied as a result of a burglary just a few weeks prior. I found the female in the back room with her hand holding her arm trying to hold the blood in. I grabbed a towel to wrap her arm and held it until EMS arrived. The whole time I was holding her arm, I was thinking, *I wish I had gloves.* I was thinking, *Do I have any cuts or scratches on my hands?* I was thinking, *That's a nice big TV, probably about 52 inches or so.*

As EMS arrived and took over the situation, I took a photo of the TV and its serial number. I couldn't investigate this matter, as I did not have a warrant or permission to search the residence. The entry was incidental to the incident and so covered by the good faith and plain view law. As she went to the hospital, I contacted the burglary office, who were quite interested in a burglar who returns previously stolen items. P.S. I made it out of this incident without a low T-cell count.

17

The Slickest Lawyer

The use of children in the commission of a crime is now more common than ever. How many times have you seen movies and heard stories of a juvenile taking the charge for an adult because the juvenile will get a lesser charge? Even I didn't realize how often it happens until I dealt with it myself. Sometimes, it even happens with parental consent. There are few crimes committed greater than when a parent does not do everything within their power to protect their child. There is no higher priority than your child. However, if this is not a child and instead a chess piece, a pawn, in particular, the sacrifice may not be the worst move to make. It works. Although it does enter the juvenile into an adult world with the mindset that juvenile penalties will apply. Still, the pawn's job is to benefit the king.

I love when reality mirrors television. I like when a clever situation on television unfolds in the span of an hour to have twists and turns. The show being designed to throw you off and lead you in the opposite direction is why it's a show. However, this is real life. It will not be wrapped up in an hour. There will be lasting consequences, and we can be certain all of the cast won't return in the sequel.

I had a call out, not unlike any other call out. I was a violent crimes detective. It was late one evening (it usually is) just as I was about to get off for the night. I got the callout saying a victim was in the hospital suffering from multiple gunshot wounds to the back. Uniformed patrol officers secured the scene. The scene was a hospital parking lot where the victim had driven his vehicle after being shot. Upon my arrival, I was advised the victim was suffering from two shots to the back, but they were non-life-threatening. In the parking lot, we found the vehicle the victim had been driving riddled with holes starting from the driver-side rear door all the way around to the rear side of the vehicle. The vehicle had a total of nine holes in it. Luckily, the victim had only been struck twice. The vehicle was taken from the parking lot and stored to be processed at a later time. When processed later, crime scene techs would go into the vehicle seats and door panels. They would cut whatever they have to cut to get the evidence that had buried itself in the deepest, most obscure innards of the vehicle. I really hate this part because we are further damaging the victim's car, but it is a necessary evil. The rounds have to be located if there is any chance of matching the bullets to the gun. Of course, I followed the vehicle to the shed to ensure that the vehicle was locked away safe and that no one came into contact with it between here and there. I had to make sure the evidence was not tainted. After securing the vehicle, I went into the hospital to contact the victim.

The victim, who advised he knew who shot him, said he did not know the actual address, but he had been shot in the 3200 block of Evangeline Street, and it was in front of a green house. The victim advised that he had driven past his girlfriend's baby daddy's house. The victim advised when he passed, he saw the baby daddy outside with a couple of other guys. The victim said he saw the baby daddy begin shooting at him and then step out in the street. Even after he passed, the baby daddy continued firing. The victim said that he kept driving and once he realized he was shot, he drove himself to the hospital. Upon identifying the baby daddy, I then put together a photographic lineup consisting of the baby daddy and five other males with similar complexion and facial features. The victim positively identified the baby daddy as the person who shot him and his vehicle.

While I was in the hospital, I had uniformed patrol officers go to the scene to secure any evidence that may have been available on scene. Uniformed patrol officers advised they were unable to locate any casings or any evidence that would say the shooting took place where the victim advised. It was currently "O dark thirty" (late night and dark), so it was entirely possible the officers simply could not locate the actual scene because it was dark. Perhaps the victim was mistaken in his identifying the location. Either way, the story had holes in it, so I would not put out a warrant for the baby daddy just yet. There were also some variables that didn't make much sense after speaking with the victim.

Previously, the victim advised he and the baby daddy had been having an ongoing feud over the baby mamma. The victim was currently in a relationship with the baby mamma. The vehicle that was damaged as a result of this shooting belonged to the baby mamma, purchased by the baby daddy. The new boyfriend was driving around in the car the ex-boyfriend bought. That's never good.

The victim had holes in the side of his car and the back. Filling in the blanks myself, I would say the driver either stopped or made multiple passes. I would say this because if the shooter did not know he was coming, he would have only been able to shoot the back of the vehicle. I was unable to speak with the victim again that night because he had gone into surgery.

The next morning, or rather, a few hours later, I went out to the scene for a daylight canvass of the area. Perhaps I could find something uniformed officers were not able to locate in the dark. I didn't find anything. As part of a daylight canvass, I knocked on all of the neighbors' doors to see if perhaps any of the neighbors saw anything. I especially like to do it with the older folks. The older folks tend to know what's going on. I spoke with one of the neighbors who advised that he had not seen the actual shooting but did see a male come out after the shooting. The anonymous neighbor stated, "that little bastard," came out and picked up every bullet off that ground. The old-timer couldn't tell me who picked up the casings but stated that he threw them in the drainage about twenty yards up the road. I left the scene and came back out about an hour later with the proper equipment to open the drainage system. As sure as he stated, I found thirteen forty-caliber casings in the drain.

The next step was to get a warrant for the baby daddy signed by a judge and get a warrant to search the residence to possibly find that gun.

I got the warrant for the baby daddy signed by the judge, no problem. The judge deemed my probable cause sufficient. Upon attempting to get a search warrant for the residence, I found that there was already a warrant written for the residence by homicide in an unrelated matter. The house was scheduled to be searched for the same thing I was looking for. That work was already done for me. It was scheduled to be searched within the week.

The baby daddy was located the next day. He was booked into Parish Prison on my warrant by a uniformed patrol officer (love those guys). I contacted the baby daddy at the Parish Prison and read him his rights per Miranda. He advised me he had nothing to say to me, which was his right. Homicide searched the house and located the forty-caliber Glock handgun in a fourteen-year-old juvenile's room. The casings were matched up to the weapon and verified. Two days passed, and the baby daddy called me at my office to tell me he wanted to make a statement. Usually, I don't play those games because now he has had a few days in

Parish Prison to formulate a story that makes sense. I went, and the baby daddy told me he couldn't hold it any longer and that it was not him who had shot the man. He advised that the person who had done the shooting was his nephew. I had seen this before. He'd made a few calls home and learned the weapon had been found in his nephew's room. He told me the fourteen-year-old juvenile nephew would confess.

Now, I was no rookie. I know the baby daddy had been arrested numerous times for similar crimes, and he had recently gotten out of prison after doing a couple years. I was aware the last thing he would want to do would be to go back to jail so soon. I couldn't just ignore the possibility he was telling the truth. I planned to contact the nephew in a couple days (I was working other cases). The nephew contacted me a day or so later. It was a Friday. I advised the nephew to come into the office on Monday. I spoke with his parents and advised them they needed to come into the office with him.

On Monday afternoon, mom, dad, and nephew came into the office. I spoke with the parents privately to explain the entire situation. The parents stood there quietly. I explained to them that the nephew's confession would not immediately free the baby daddy, and it may not free him at all. I explained to the parents their juvenile son might be about to confess to a felony he did not commit to save his uncle who had already done other crimes, some similar to this one. The parents were still quiet.

Okay, we all sit down in the interview room, cameras rolling. I read the fourteen-year-old juvenile nephew his rights per Miranda directly from a rights waiver form. The form lists the rights individually and requires initials by each right to prove they were read and understood. Being that I was working with a fourteen-year-old, I read the rights slowly and deliberately. I asked the nephew if he understood. Then, I asked the mom and the dad if they understood before moving on to the next right. Each person acknowledged they understood every right verbally. The juvenile signed. Then, the mother and the father signed the form.

The nephew began his confession. He told me that he had been one of the persons standing outside on the night the event occurred. The nephew advised he had the gun, and he recognized the car when it passed by the first time. The nephew said when the vehicle passed the second time, he began to shoot. He said he shot multiple times. The nephew advised he walked out in the street shooting at the car. I asked him why he would do such a thing. He advised that he thought the driver was going to make the block and shoot at them. I asked him where his uncle was during this encounter, and he advised the uncle ducked behind a car. The nephew confessed to every aspect of the crime. I placed the nephew into juvenile detention. And as I told him, the baby daddy remained in prison.

Adult prisoners take a while to actually go to trial. The juvenile system operates much faster. Two months later, give or take, the juvenile was on trial. I received a subpoena to come to court. When I went to court, the lawyer was dressed in a cream-colored tweed suit with a matching hat. He had a blue bow tie. I will remember him forever. He had a pleasant appearance. The lawyer called me up to the stand and asked me if I had read the juvenile his rights. Of course, I said I had. He asked me if he understood them.

I told him, "Yes, I'm certain he understood them."

The lawyer said, "On what grounds do you place your belief that this fourteen-year-old understood his rights?"

I replied, "I don't understand the question."

"Haven't you met adults that did not understand their rights?"

"Yes, I have."

"Are you still sure this fourteen-year-old child understood his rights?"

"I read them slowly and explained each right in a manner that I think he could understand."

"Is it still possible he didn't understand?"

"Yes, it is possible, but unlikely."

"Why is it unlikely?"

"Because I did it in the presence of his mother and father."

"Did the parents understand the rights?"

"Yes, they did."

"How do you know?"

"They signed a waiver saying they understood after I explained the rights in a manner that a fourteen-year-old could understand."

We looked at the video, and to the prosecutor and me, it appeared that it was a perfect rights waiver signing. Both the prosecutor and I were completely satisfied that the nephew and the parents understood their rights and had signed the waiver knowing full well what it meant. But alas, the judge eventually ruled that the juvenile did not understand his rights. This meant that the confession could no longer be admitted as evidence. Without the confession, the rest of the case was circumstantial. So, as a byproduct, this case was dismissed.

The most important part of this is the nephew never had to take the stand. Therefore, he never recanted his confession. What significance is this? When the uncle went to trial a while later, the juvenile's confession was presented as evidence. If someone else confessed to the crime, how can the baby daddy be guilty? Case dismissed!

This case is proof that you can do everything right and still fail.

18

Should a Man Have to Take a Beating?

One of the most inexhaustible misconceptions about police is that they are cowards who were beaten up in school. They were beaten, felt small as a result and are now out to take their revenge on the world. This is a projection of that 0.00001 percent. So, yeah, that guy is out there. But he is not this guy.

It should be hard to believe a police officer could be a coward. Think for a minute of the big badass officer surrounded by other officers. He can go anywhere and say anything. He has backup. This is the perception. The reality is totally the opposite. In most places, officers ride one officer to a vehicle. This is mainly because resources are limited. The more units on the street, the more officer presence is felt by the populous at large. Most officers tend to ride with a partner nearby, or they go to calls together whenever they can. This is not always possible. A much more common situation is the officer is alone out in a situation that would cause most people to wet themselves.

I have learned from experience that I am not a coward. Until the situation had arisen, I could only assume. I have seen civilians wet themselves, freeze during a violent situation or behave in an otherwise irrational way. Most of the time, the cowards among the departments are weeded out in the first two years. We've had plenty of people get into shootings or fistic encounters and quit shortly thereafter. I'm not saying all of these officers are cowards; some just realized this work is not for them. No one looks upon these people as less. We are simply thankful that they got out alive and did not cost someone else their life.

As a detective, as previously stated, decisions have to be made; decisions that have lasting effects on other people. Sometimes, a difference of opinion doesn't translate to something good. I often have debates with my coworkers and supervisors about a case. These debates are not pointless. They allow us to look at cases from different angles. Sometimes, it is impossible to take yourself out of a certain point of view without someone else's opinion. There is a particular case that stands out. We have had this debate numerous times and relate other cases to it. The case involved a situation that, in my opinion, could have been handled two ways with both ways being right. The difference is that everyone is not built for fistic encounters. And if you know you are not built for a fight, then why engage in one? It's basically asking for a beating.

I'm on call and its 12 o'clock in the morning. The phone rings, and I'm advised that we have a man down from a gunshot wound to the leg. It would seem to be a pretty minor call. The suspect was still on scene. The victim is being transported to the hospital. I go to the scene. While I'm on scene, I've got a lot of blood in the grass and one casing on the ground near the blood. I have a couple of witnesses, including the suspect. Usually, I wouldn't have even been called out if they had the suspect on scene. What was different in this situation? A witness advised me that this is what happened: Pam was at her residence with her husband and her two little girls. Her ex-husband came by to pick up his two little girls so that they can spend the weekend with him. The ex-husband came to the door to get the kids. The kids, who were happy to see their father, went out and got into his van. The current husband was in the house, keeping his distance. The current husband and the ex-husband had a history. They had violence between them because of Pam and the kids. To avoid any trouble, they had since then avoided each other.

Pam stood outside and spoke with the ex-husband. That was the last information the current husband could provide about what occurred outside. The next bit of information he had was he heard a commotion. The current husband looked out of the window to see the ex-husband on top of Pam, punching her. The current husband made his way downstairs with his handgun. Upon coming into contact with the ex-husband, he shot the ex-husband. He fired one time, hitting the ex-husband in the leg. He pulled his wife away from the ex-husband and called the police and an ambulance. Pam suffered only minor bruises as a result of the battery.

As messed up as this situation seems, you would think it would be cut and dry, would you not? You are more than entitled to protect your land and property. You are even more inclined to protect your family. It would seem reasonable that he shot the person who was actively attacking his wife. He shot the assailant once, stopped the threat and contacted help for the bad guy. What more could you ask for?

Well, let me start by repeating the discussion I've been having in my office from that date to this one. Why did the current husband not fight the ex-husband? Was he at liberty to use deadly force? What I mean to ask is: If his wife was not in life-threatening danger, could the current husband actually use deadly force? Please make no mistake that anytime a firearm is used, it constitutes deadly force.

My argument is everyone can't fight, or rather, everyone is not a fighter. Why should this man (the current husband) engage in a possible fisticuff with a man whom he knows to be violent?

How can we verify that this was a life or death situation if the victim Pam, only received minor bruises? Perhaps the current husband arrived in time to prevent such actions. My co-worker's point of view is that the husband should have physically attacked the ex-husband because the ex-husband had no weapon. I would argue, how would the ex-husband know for certain. The husband could have been hurt or killed himself, and that, of course, wouldn't have helped his wife, now would it?

After days of debating, the husband was charged with second-degree aggravated battery. Being the wife only suffered minor injuries, the ex-husband was only charged with simple battery. I can't say I was happy with the outcome. If it were up to me, the current husband would have gotten a high five and sent on his way. Fortunately, in these situations, the arrest is not the final word. When the current husband went to court, all charges were dropped.

19

From Kidnapping to Simple Battery

Cops can be cynical. This is a statement I'm sure most civilians can probably agree with. I am doubly sure that most cops will agree as well. The reason could be because we (police) see some horrible things. I am inclined to think it's because we see how the system fails. This is not the case all the time. Sometimes, we are disappointed to find out that justice is not always served. I rarely take anything personally. This is just my career slash job. The things that are important to me are kept at home. I don't play these things close to the collar. I do the best job I am capable of, and most times, we get the bad guy to where he needs to be. On occasion, the ball has been dropped for whatever reason. Perhaps I couldn't find the witness who saw the whole thing. Perhaps the witness didn't want to get involved. Whatever the case may be, all I can do is my best.

I have not always been this way. When I first started, I was a person who was going to make a difference. I would go out and do great things, and when I was done, the neighborhood, the city and the world would be better for it. Over time, the gloss from my badge has dimmed quite a bit. The excitement has faded away, and the roar of motivation has simmered down to a light hum.

It's not really the small cases that take away your motivation. It's the ones you remember and required more effort on your part.

On one warm summer midnight, I received a call that advised there was a female who had been kidnapped. The suspect was thought to be her boyfriend. The victim had been taken away from the scene and could no longer be contacted. I was contacted and responded. These cases are common. I've dealt with this kind of thing on more than a few occasions. The main thing is gathering information. If we know the suspect, then we can find out where he hangs out and where his friends are.

I immediately came to the scene where the female was taken. I spoke with a witness who advised the suspect was her ex-boyfriend, and the victim was his new girlfriend. The witness was reluctant to talk to police. After a lot of coaxing, I found out the witness had been a victim of the suspect in the past. The current witness was the suspect's ex-girlfriend. She had been with the suspect for approximately ten years. She told me that she and the suspect had two children together. She advised me the suspect was very abusive, and she had suffered many beatings at his hands. She told me she had escaped in a manner of speaking. She had been separated from the suspect for approximately two years and had no wish to get back involved with him in any way, shape or fashion. After checking the police database, I found there were a bunch of cases involving the witness and the suspect. I congratulated the witness on her escape. It was a sincere congratulation because of the difficult nature of getting out of a toxic relationship.

That being said, I told her I really needed the details of this incident. After building a level of rapport, I was able to get her to tell me what transpired. The witness advised at around 12:00 am, she received a knock on the door. The witness advised it was the victim. She had come to the residence and said she was there to pick up the suspect and witness' son. The victim whispered to the witness, "Please let me in. I need to call someone to pick me up."

The witness said the victim appeared as if she had been battered. Her hair was a mess, and she had bruises and scratches on her face. The witness advised she wanted no part of this scenario. She advised she did not want the victim to come into the house and that her son was not at the residence. She advised that her son was with her daughter. The witness advised, the suspect then ran past her and came into her house.

The victim then quickly closed the door. The victim advised she simply wanted to call a ride to come and get her because the suspect was beating her. The victim called the witness and the suspect's daughter to come and pick her up. Shortly after this incident, the suspect came and began beating on the door. The victim begged the witness not to open the door. The witness advised she waited but eventually opened the door because she knew the suspect well and did not want to become a victim herself. The witness advised the victim immediately tried to run out the back door. The suspect came into the residence, uninvited, and went straight for the victim. The suspect grabbed the victim and punched her repeatedly. The suspect then forcibly drug her out of the residence. As the suspect cursed and drug the victim back to his vehicle, the suspect's daughter arrived in her car. The suspect's son got out of his sister's car leaving the passenger's door open. The victim was able to get away from the suspect momentarily. The victim then ran and jumped into the car with the daughter. Startled and in a panic, the daughter drove away with the victim in the car. The suspect ran to his car and followed his daughter.

The witness advised her daughter returned to the residence a short time later. When the daughter returned, her passenger side window was broken. The daughter then called the police. This was all the information the witness could provide.

I spoke to the daughter, who was still on scene. The daughter advised she was at her residence when she received a call from her mother's house. The phone hung up before she could get an understanding of what was going on. The daughter advised she was about to bring her brother to the residence anyway, so it was no big deal. She assumed that was what the call was about anyway. The trip was a short one, and so she went.

She advised that, upon her arrival, she stopped the car, and her brother got out. She advised as soon as he did, her father's girlfriend, to whom she was a friend, jumped in the car. The victim started yelling at her to "DRIVE! DRIVE! DRIVE!" The daughter advised she drove almost immediately out of instinct. She advised she soon realized that her father was in pursuit. The daughter said that she knew her father quite well and wanted no part of this incident. She said her father pulled up on the side of her vehicle while in his vehicle, which actually belonged to the victim.

The suspect was attempting to flag her down. She advised the suspect, her father, then fell back in the vehicle. The daughter advised the suspect, her father, rear-ended her vehicle then pulled up on the side of her vehicle. The daughter said her father, the suspect, yelled at her to stop and then promptly pulled ahead of her. The suspect then put his car in a position in front of his daughter's car causing her to stop and be unable to move forward. The suspect then walked over to the passenger's side of the vehicle where the victim was seated and told her to get out of the car. The victim locked the door and refused to get out of the vehicle. The suspect then located a brick and broke the passenger window out as the victim tried to scramble to the backseat to avoid being captured. The victim eventually gave up and came out of the vehicle. The daughter advised her father, the suspect, then placed the victim into the passenger seat of her (the victim's) vehicle and drove away. The daughter returned to her mother's house and called the police.

We had a description of the car and the address of the victim.

I sent an officer there, but the vehicle was not there. Officers knocked on the door. Neither the suspect nor the victim was there. We checked all of the residences that we thought might be affiliated with the victim or the suspect. After checking a lot of locations, one officer passed back by the original address of the victim. The vehicle was spotted at the address. Officers attempted to contact the victim and suspect who were presumably inside the residence. Since no one would answer the door, we could not simply enter the residence. Because we could hear movement inside the residence, I drew up a warrant for entry into the residence. SWAT surrounded the residence and prepared to make entry. After jumping through all the hoops required for a warrant, I delivered the warrant to the scene. Just as SWAT prepared to make entry, the suspect attempted to climb out of a hole in the wall at the back of the residence. The suspect was taken into custody.

Upon interviewing the victim, she advised that she had had an argument with the suspect, her live-in boyfriend, the previous day at around 3:00 pm. The victim advised that she had questioned the suspect about another female whom he had been conversing with, and he "lost it." The victim advised he started beating her in the house with her kids, so she ran outside. The suspect then forced her in the car, and they left the house. They left children, all under twelve years of age, in the house until about 3:00 am. The two rode around for hours with the suspect sporadically punching the victim whenever the mood struck. He had taken her all around the city never allowing her to leave his sight until he went to his ex-girlfriend's house to pick up his son. The victim suffered only minor injuries, physically—minor being construed as no broken bones. However, there was a black eye, a few knots, scrapes and some bruises.

The suspect was charged with kidnapping, false imprisonment, simple battery, domestic abuse battery, home invasion, child endangerment, aggravated criminal damage to property, simple criminal damage to property, hit and run, careless operation, unauthorized use of a motor vehicle and domestic abuse by strangulation.

That's twelve charges, all valid, no railroading occurring. The facts of the case would be easy to prove. I had the statement of the witnesses and victims recorded. A big problem with domestic abuse cases is the nature of relationships. By the time the case was brought to trial, the couple was back together. They were friends again. People don't tend to do things that get their friends in trouble. No matter how misguided and self-destructive this behavior may seem, this scenario is a common thing.

Approximately two months later, my supervisor tells me he has seen my case with my victims at trial. These cases never go to trial so fast. The most used tactic by lawyers is to delay the case. I think, save for juvenile cases, I have never seen any case go to court short of eight months. Here we have a very complicated case with twelve charges pending, and it's in court two months later without the lead detective even so much as having been subpoenaed. My supervisor told me the suspect, the big bad bully who clearly committed so many wrongs, pled to simple battery. Simple battery: A simple battery occurs when a person makes intentional contact of an insulting or provoking nature with the person of another. Simple battery is a misdemeanor that carries a maximum of six months in jail and/or a fine of 500 dollars.

I would assume there was a reason this case was cleared with little more than a slap on the wrist. I'm sure there was secret information passed around in exchange for leniency. I can't be certain it was worth it. I should have at least gotten to discuss this exchange.

20

Bloody Mess

A death is always a tragic scenario often made worse by the age of the victim. It is always sad when someone dies. In my opinion, it's a tragedy when someone young dies both prematurely and unnecessarily. When I come to a homicide scene, I have to put my personal opinions to the side. The facts are all that matter. The major reason to keep your personal opinion separate is that it will lead you astray. When you come to a scene there is not a person lying on the ground. There is only evidence. You need to treat it as such. At the same time, you need to appear to the family to treat the body as if it's someone's loved one. The contradiction of the ideas is difficult to get past, but it's a line we tread daily.

An example of your personal opinion leading you astray is the death of a prostitute. When you find out the female is a prostitute, you may immediately jump to drugs or a john. If you are looking for these things, you may miss the fact that she hasn't been involved in that kind of life since her last arrest a year or more prior. The circumstances may be completely unaffiliated with that lifestyle or circumstances. However, when I check the police reports and find out about her past, that's where you start to look. It's not impossible you will find your way back. It is a detour that is a waste of time and resources, not to mention that if you look hard enough for a thing you usually find it.

Having made the speech about keeping preconceived notions out of it, let me contradict myself. When coming on the scene of a homicide, the detective will draw on all of his previous experience to make sense of the scene.

I received a call at around three in the morning. It's always three in the morning. Nothing bad ever happens at a decent hour. I was advised we had what appeared to be a homicide. The victim appeared to have been shot at his residence with a shotgun. I was advised this was possibly an attempted robbery. This was a horrible cluster, so I will try to describe the scene as best I can.

I arrived at the scene, a small house. It was a very cold day. This is not a common occurrence down south. We are not used to very cold days. There was a layer of ice on the ground. When I say ice, I mean a thin layer of frost. The yard was cut and appeared to be well-groomed. There was a large track across the yard as if a vehicle had just made the indentations and rolled across a soft part of the yard. The indentation appeared to have been recent because the frosty dew was not inside of the indentation, but you could see the water was starting to freeze in the newly created puddle.

The house had a door on the front of the residence facing the road and one on the left side. Both doors had three concrete stairs in front of them because the house was lifted approximately three feet off the ground (also common down south). The left side of the house had a one-car awning. The side door was located at the back of the left side of the residence but still under the awning. The front door was slightly ajar, and the side door was even more so. I could see through the windows and the doors that all of the lights were on inside of the residence. I could see the feet, legs and pants of the obvious victim through the side door. The side door led directly into the kitchen. I could hear a lot of noise inside of the residence. After listening for a moment, I could tell it was the television. Before entering the residence, I took a walk around the outside of the residence. I note that I was a rookie investigator at the time of this case. This was possibly my fourth homicide, but it was okay because I had seen hundreds of movies about them (sarcasm). Upon walking around the residence, I didn't notice much, except a back window that seemed out of place. I noticed the window was opened about an inch. The blinds appeared to be in disarray. The blinds were those old school metal blinds that, once bent, could never be straightened again. I could see there were a few that were bent badly. However, I would note the ground outside the window was undisturbed. The frost on the ground was still...frosty.

Upon my return to the front of the residence, I decided to go in through the side. I needed to go through before crime scene went through just to get a layout of the scene. I could see the victim lying on the floor just beside the door but not blocking the door's movement. Upon entering, the victim was laid out feet toward the door with head facing away. He was on his back. He had a 9mm handgun in his left hand with an extended magazine. His finger was still on the trigger. His eyes were slightly open. His feet were crossed, and his pants were down around his ankles. The victim had boxers on with...himself exposed through the boxer hole. The victim was lying in a large pool of blood. Also, the victim was young, too young to ever be in a situation like this.

If you were to enter the residence through the side door, you would be in a small kitchen. Immediately to the left, you would see some cabinets and a kitchen sink. Approximately fifteen feet directly across from the door was a washing machine. To the right of that washing machine was a door that led to a bathroom. There was a refrigerator in the room about eight feet inside the door to the right. Immediately to the right of the door, which opened on the left side, hinged to the right, there was an opening to the rest of the house. The rest of the house consisted of two more rooms, the living room, and a bedroom.

The victim had obviously been shot numerous times. My original thought was he had been shot with a shotgun loaded with buckshot. Due to the amount of blood and position of the body, it was impossible to say how many times he had been hit. At the time, I was only certain that it had been multiple shots. Upon closer inspection, it became clear the victim had not been shot with a shotgun but had actually been shot a lot of times. It appeared he was shot with a handgun. We would have to wait until the autopsy to get any confirmation. There were footprints through the pools of blood. The blood had been tracked throughout the little house. There was an assortment of footprints leading in and out of the residence. There were multiple footprints, multiple shoe types and multiple shoe sizes. There was money scattered around the room as well, a lot of money. There were ones, tens, twenties and even hundred-dollar bills. Some of the money was covered in blood. The incident, or whatever had occurred, may not have started in the kitchen. The kitchen was where it culminated.

I could see there were bullets in the floor. I could see there were bullets in the walls and ceiling. I could see there was a trail of bullets leading from the floor to the wall all the way up to the ceiling.

Upon leaving the kitchen and entering the living room, I could see there was a television that was, or rather had been, sitting on a stand. The stand and television had been knocked over and were now facing the floor. There were RCA cables that were plugged into the back of the television. The cables did not appear to be attached to anything. I was thinking perhaps the DVD player had been stolen during...whatever this was. The chairs in the room were all knocked over. There was a single couch, and it was knocked over. There was the distinct smell of marijuana in the residence. Upon a closer look, there were baggies of crack on the floor. I would note that all around the room were pictures. The pictures were of children and adults. The pictures were old pictures with that reddish color that was all the rage in the late 1970s and early 1980s. There were little figurines on all the shelves: cats, dogs and little cherubim angels. The residence was decorated as if it belonged to an old person. The furniture was outdated. The house was bursting with items. It gave the impression a person's entire life was packed into this small apartment.

The little house had one bedroom. The bedroom decor matched the rest of the house. The room was small and packed with a lot of items but was neat. Nothing had been thrown around the room. There was a small amount of crack cocaine in a makeshift pipe. It was clear the person had been about to smoke it. This is a rarity. It had to be a sudden event because connoisseurs of crack cocaine are rarely interrupted from their favorite endeavor. There were also a bunch of figurines all through the bedroom, consistent with the rest of the house. The figurines of dogs, cats and angels were ever-present. The residence had the feel of an elderly woman who lived alone. The television was playing a porno video with the volume turned up.

The briefing from the uniformed officers advised, when they had received a call saying shots were fired at this location, they arrived promptly to see no vehicles in the yard. The officers advised both doors were open. The officers advised upon their arrival they heard someone inside, apparently screaming for help. They went inside the residence to both clear it and render aid if needed. The officers advised the residence was empty save for the victim. The officers advised the only thing they disturbed was the bathroom door, which was closed when they arrived. I could see the path that the officers had taken due to the blood on the floor and the large number of footprints. I could see there had been so much traffic inside the residence that it would be impossible to tell who had come or gone or how many people were in the residence. They also advised the cries for help came from the TV.

This was clearly a bloody mess. I could only guess what occurred at this time. To give you an understanding of where my mind was at the time, I will give you my original hypothesis. I imagined the victim was at his grandmother's house. I assumed she was not home at the time, and it was just the victim there. I figured he had a beef with someone, and he knew it. He may have gone to his grandmother's residence because he figured they would not expect to find him there. I assumed his grandmother was out of town because there was a porno playing, loudly, and crack in the house. Grandmas tend to frown on that behavior. I think there was a loud noise or something that caught his attention, suddenly causing him to jump up and try to see what happened. He already knew he had someone after him, so he had his firearm ready. Maybe he was in the middle of some self-love prior to the disturbance. Maybe someone got in the house. When he ran to see what it was, he was attacked. There were more people than he thought. He fought. That's it. That's all I had, and as you can see, quite thin.

We had to find his grandmother. We had to identify him. The fingerprints were being matched. We found out the person to whom the house belonged. She was an older woman who lived alone. She was indeed out of town and had been for months. She had no grandkids. No one was supposed to be in her house. However, she did give a key to a friend, a middle-aged man who cut her grass. She advised she had given him the key to her house to watch it while she was gone. He was her maintenance man. We had to find him. While going over the scene with a fine-toothed comb, I noticed something else. It was a tiny camera that was just to the left of the door. At the time, it was the tiniest camera I had ever seen. It was hidden in a small decorative frog coming out of the wall. Upon closer inspection, there were wires coming from the wall that ran all the way to the living room and out the wall to the knocked over television. We had not noticed the wires before because of the mess. It appears a DVD player was not stolen. Perhaps it was a recording device.

A camera at the door didn't make the owner of the house a criminal, but it didn't seem like the thing an older person would be up on. I have a grandmother, and it took her many years to get on the Internet. I'm still trying to get her to get into Facebook.

Upon speaking to the owner of the house, she advised that she did have a camera, but it was only connected to the television. There was no recording device stolen.

The victim was identified as a local kid who lived in the area. He has an extensive history of robbery.

Upon finally locating the makeshift maintenance man, we had a few questions. We found out, first, that it was a bad idea to leave your key with someone like this guy. After that, though, we found out the maintenance man had what was called a strip party. He was at a local strip club and decided after closing that he wanted to keep the party going. He invited some of the ladies back to "his house." He also invited a few of his friends to come. You see, the ladies wouldn't come if there was no money to be made. He advised he did not know all of the people at the party. He had no way of contacting them. He advised most of them were just people from the club.

The maintenance man advised this is what happened....

"We were at the party having fun. Everyone was doing his or her thing. People were in and out. We could see as people came to the door because of the camera. The word got out that we were having a party, so people started showing up. The kid came to the door and knocked. We let him in. As soon as he came in, he drew a gun. When he came in, he told everyone to get on the floor. Big Boy was in the bathroom at the time. He was in there making noise, so the kid told him to 'Bring yo ass out of there.' Big Boy came into the room with a hand full of money. Big Boy said, 'Take it.' The kid said, 'Naw. It's too late.' Big Boy threw the money up and grabbed the kid and the gun. We all started running. By the time I made it to the front yard, I heard shots, lots of shots."

The maintenance man said he didn't know any of the people at the party. He didn't know their names. He knew that the girls worked at the strip club. He knew the guys happened to be in the strip club when he was there.

Being that so many shots were heard, we called hospitals, all of them. We got a call back from one that was very far off. They had a victim who had been shot in the…testicles, actually just the left one. I asked the nurse, who was so kind to call me back, what was the build of this poor specimen. The nurse paused and said, "He's a big boy."

Upon speaking with Big Boy, he was read his rights per Miranda. I didn't think he committed murder, but he had left the scene and didn't call for help. Big Boy advised he heard when the kid came into the house and told everyone to get on the floor. He eventually advised he was in the bathroom snorting cocaine. Big Boy advised when he heard the kid, he tried to climb out of the window. The window was nailed shut, and he could not get out. He said he slipped on the tub trying to raise the window and made noise. Big Boy said he heard the kid say, "Come yo ass out of there." Big Boy said he grabbed all the money he had to give to the kid. He came out the bathroom and attempted to give him the money. He advised the kid said it was too late and pointed the gun at him. Big Boy then said some very, very important words. "I thought he was going to kill me," which is another way of saying I was in fear for my life. Big Boy advised he threw the money in the air and grabbed the gun. Big Boy said that's when everyone left him. Big Boy said he grabbed the gun and the kid fought. He advised he was much bigger than the kid, but the kid still fought hard. The kid began to shoot. The gun was aimed at the ceiling. Big Boy said as he tried to get the gun out of the kid's hand. The kid repeatedly fired at the ceiling, then at the wall and then at the floor. Big Boy said his hand was on the gun, but the kid was pulling the trigger. Big Boy said he was trying to turn the gun back toward the kid so he would stop shooting. Big Boy said somewhere in the process, the gun was aimed at his crotch, and he was shot. Big Boy said the kid was hit multiple times but continued firing. Big Boy said that after he (Big Boy) was shot, he became weak and would have lost his life if not for the kid's pants. The kid's pants fell around his ankles during the fight. He could not maintain his balance. Big Boy said the kid shot himself as they fell to the floor. Big Boy said the gun kept firing as they wrestled on the floor. Big Boy said as soon as the gun stopped firing, he ran outside, got into his car and left. He couldn't say if the kid was alive when he left.

Big Boy advised he did not go to a local hospital because of the circumstances. He had been doing drugs. Big Boy said he didn't know what to do. He panicked and kept driving. Big Boy said he never planned to go to the hospital but realized he had no choice. He said he didn't want anyone to ask any questions, so he drove to an out-of-town hospital.

This was clearly self-defense. Big Boy, in his sheer ignorance and propensity for being involved in unsavory hobbies, made a bad situation worse. If we had not found him when we did, he could have been charged with murder. I know you likely think this would have been an open and shut case, but it's not.

The fact that Big Boy was already involved in criminal activities is a factor. The fact that everyone ran out, leaving just the two of them in the house, was a factor. The fact that he left town to avoid dealing with the situation was a significant factor.

Big Boy was not charged.

I learned there are unlimited scenarios in unlimited situations. I had no idea what had happened and could have never guessed it would end up as a self-defense case. This was a terrible case to have but one that taught me in the worst possible way never to come with preconceived notions. I now go to every case with an open mind.

21

Police Encounters

When I go out and speak with a class or any group of people as an officer, the conversation has certain characteristics. The circumstances may change slightly with each conversation, but the main theme remains the same. I will give my spill about what I do as an officer, and then I ask, are there any questions? I get a barrage of: "Why do police do this?" and "Why do police do that?" I defend the honor of officers everywhere as best I can. I eventually get to the point where I start asking for volunteers. I say, "Hey, why don't you come fill out an application." The initial response depends on the crowd.

If I am speaking to the average crowd, there are chants of: "Its too dangerous." "You don't get paid enough." I couldn't agree more. If I am speaking to a minority crowd (of which I am a member), I usually get, "Hell no. You have to put up with too much." "Hell no, I'm no sell out." I confront this argument with a standard statement. How can you expect to be treated fairly by an organization of which you have no representation? This is a normal thought, in my opinion.

One day, while I was speaking with my wife, we were having a debate. We discussed the proper way to deal with an officer during an encounter. She says she has never had a bad encounter with a police officer. I tell her I have had numerous bad encounters with police. The difference could be as simple as she is a woman, and I am a man. I would venture to say that there are other variables that we have not considered. We are both minorities, which statistically tend to have a larger number of bad encounters with police.

My wife was raised in a small town, really small. Seriously though, they only have one street light. Things that are different in a small town compared to city are everywhere. In a small town, everyone knows each other. When she was stopped as a teenager, the officer who stopped her knew who she was, likely even knew who her father was. She, in kind, would likely know the officer as well, if not personally, perhaps he worked at her school or as security at the newly built Walmart. My point being there was no fear associated with the stop. She had no fear beyond possibly getting grounded for speeding. She knew better than to compound the violation by being rude or disobeying the officer. If she was disrespectful, its likely her parents would have known pretty quickly.

This is something my wife carried into her adulthood. She was comfortable in dealing with law enforcement. She was not a victim of the paralyzing fear that some people are afflicted with during a stop. She was also not affected by the anger that afflicts some people. She was raised in an environment where she was taught respect for the police. As a result of this upbringing, she hasn't had a bad encounter with police.

Another factor is, every time she has been stopped, she was guilty (her own admittance) because she knew she was speeding or swerving or whatever. While she is not an expert in the law, she felt comfortable enough to allow things to proceed. When she was stopped, she didn't figure the officer was out to get her. She thought the officers were simply doing their job. When she came into contact with the officer, she acted accordingly. Perhaps this is why she has never had a bad experience. Plus, she's pretty.

On the other hand, I have grown up in neighborhoods that are only a small part of a large city. Nearly every encounter I have had with the police was a negative one. The stops were always done by someone who was a stranger to me. Still worse, I would get stopped by the same officer from a previous bad experience. There was never an opportunity to build any rapport. The stop was always done by someone who was not a part of the majority of that neighborhood. Like my wife, I was not well versed in the law or its function. I had been taught the police were the bad guys. I didn't know anything about them, and I had heard they would beat you.

As a result, when I was stopped, I was nervous. My hands shook. My words did not come smoothly. What does a nervous teenager look like to you? I can tell you what it looks like to a police officer. It looks like he is hiding something, or perhaps he is guilty of something. The look is likely the same as a drug dealer with drugs in his pocket. I'd be sweating and fidgety. Because I was twitchy, the officer would be overly cautious. He would likely search me. I would be offended because, in my eyes, I was just harassed. How can this guy just come into my neighborhood and go in my pockets? In my mind, it was the same as someone robbing me of my dignity. Because police tend to patrol minority neighborhoods more often, these encounters happened pretty often. I was never found with any drugs or anything of that nature, but these encounters shaped my opinion of officers. Obviously, I didn't like them.

Not all my encounters with police officers were bad. There was the occasional officer who would come and talk to my school or come to the basketball court to have a conversation. There were enough of these times to make me understand that each officer was his own person. Theses few moments allowed me to see what a police officer was supposed to be.

Of course, there were encounters with officers who were simply bad officers, assholes if you will.

I used to work at Burger King when I was sixteen years old. As a juvenile, it was the law that I was forced to take an hour break every four hours. I didn't like this because it made the other employees not like you and cut into my money. The Burger King was near my grandmother's house. The ride on my bike would take about fifteen minutes. I would ride my bike there, hang out for about thirty minutes and be back before my break was up. To get to Granny's house, I had to pass through a wealthy neighborhood. I liked riding through the neighborhood because the streets were smooth and the houses were huge. The neighborhood was patrolled by off-duty police officers working extra duty. The first day I passed through the neighborhood on my bike wearing my uniform, an officer stopped me. The officer asked me where I was going. I told him to my grandmother's house. I told him where she lived. He asked me where I was coming from. I was annoyed by the question considering I was wearing my uniform. Also, I thought both questions were none of his business. Nonetheless, I told him where I was coming from. He asked my name, where I lived and an assortment of questions. After searching me, the officer allowed me to go on my way.

I felt like he was just harassing me. I had not broken any law. I visited my grandmother and went back to work. The next day, I took the same path and was stopped again by the same officer. He asked me all the same questions. The second encounter was almost identical to the first. The main difference would be that I was more angry than afraid this time. The officer eventually allowed me to leave. I visited my grandmother and went back to work. On the ride back, I took a different path. I didn't want to come into contact with the officer again.

The third day, I went back to my grandmother's house taking the new path. I didn't see the officer. I had a good visit and all was well. About two days later, after a couple of off days, I went back to my grandmother's house. I took the new path. The officer appeared to have been waiting for me. He stopped me once again. He asked me where I was going and where I was coming from. He asked my name, date of birth, my address, etc. He made it as plain as anyone could have; he was messing with me. I asked him why he kept stopping me, and he told me that this was a dark area, and there were a lot of burglaries that occurred in the area. The officer advised I didn't look like I was from around the area. He then stated that I should avoid the area to avoid being stopped. This officer didn't want me in the neighborhood, and his actions convinced me not to return. This was a bad officer. This officer helped shape my opinion of all future officers that I encountered. I could have likely had this situation remedied after the second encounter, but due to a lack of knowledge, I did nothing and endured this harassment.

In her small town, my wife would have had this problem taken care of immediately. She would have likely told her parents the first time it happened. She would have likely been able to tell her parents who the officer was. I had no clue whom the officer I was dealing with was. He didn't have a nametag and didn't introduce himself.

I was not taught to be nonconfrontational. I was never taught not to question officers. It was and is normal for me to question authority. However, I do know when to shut up. While I am certain this will keep me from getting hurt, this also hurts my pride. As a youth, like most youths, I wanted to feel powerful. At around the age of seventeen, I was starting to actually feel powerful. I can tell you when I felt the weakest was when I was in the presence of police officers. Personally, I think this is why so many people are so confrontational with police. This is why it's always those who are minorities or poor people or just those on the fringes of society who have the largest problem with police. It's a hard thing to give up power. It is all at once the hardest thing to give up the only power, the only control you have, control of one's self. Most people, especially poor people, spend more than half their waking hours at work, likely a low-paying job working under the supervision of someone barely more qualified than they are. There you take orders. When you are off, you still aren't free, but there is a measure of freedom. When the police come, you have to surrender that small measure of freedom. Sometimes, that surrender is not easy. Sometimes, that surrender is impossible.

Think for a moment when you have seen these *YouTube* videos where the driver of a vehicle has been stopped and refuses to wind down the window. That is a refusal to surrender power. Inside their vehicle, they are in charge, so they refuse to allow in someone who will take over. What has obviously been missed is that the officer will still have to do his job.

Police get tired of having to explain perfectly legal actions to someone who does not understand the law. The experts at the *YouTube* channel told you that you didn't have to wind down the window. No doubt, this was information from some half-read explanation of their rights. That half-read explanation was then both poorly translated and even more poorly understood. What was missed is that you have been legally stopped. If you have been legally stopped, then by law, you legally have to identify yourself if requested by the officer. People forget that it is a privilege to drive, not a right. When you got that driver's license, you had to sign paperwork saying you would abide by the laws of the road. With all that said, you have to show your identification and your vehicle information.

People clearly don't read their tickets when they get them. It says clearly, "This ticket is in lieu of an arrest." That is to say, I'm giving you this ticket instead of arresting you. However, if you do not cooperate with this advantageous procedure, then what? "In lieu" doesn't work when one of two options are removed. Your only option is to be arrested. Soooo, when I'm trying to give you a ticket, but you refuse to identify yourself or sign the ticket, remember "in lieu." This includes getting belligerent with me about this exchange. The attempt to give you a ticket will be replaced with an arrest.

When was that paragraph significant in the *YouTube* videos? Well, when a person is being arrested, the procedure is far different than when they are arrested. The biggest issue is, people don't see when the traffic stop transitions to an arrest. So, when that learn-ed person is behind their window claiming they don't have to communicate with the officer, what happens? They break the bargain, and now they are under arrest. When someone gets a ticket, it is usually a back and forth. The back and forth is usually calm and collected. There are questions that are asked and actions that are requested. When it's an arrest, there are actions that are requested, yes, but those requests are actually demands. They are orders. So, if you are getting arrested and you refuse to let down the window, the window gets broken. You are removed from the vehicle. In your mind, you are being mishandled for a traffic violation. The reality is, if you refused to cooperate with the ticket, you've opted to be arrested. That would be a poor choice, to say the least.

Police are supposed to treat each stop as if it is an individual stop. What I mean to say is, if you had a bad encounter on your previous stop, it should not affect your attitude on the next stop. Unfortunately, police departments are comprised of people—air-breathing humans. They are not without flaws. If I was cursed out on the last call, it might make my nerves a little bad for the next situation. Most professional police are beyond this type of behavior. Police get used to being insulted, cursed, etc. They learn how to treat the next encounter as if the previous one didn't happen.

However, police are still human. When it comes to a situation that is filled with adrenaline, things change. What a civilian doesn't know is a traffic stop is probably the scariest situation a cop faces. He faces it on a daily basis. A traffic stop is the most likely time an officer will be killed. It's the situation he finds himself in the most. Furthermore, it's even more likely in this situation, he will be alone. Add in all the variables that come with each and every traffic stop, and you are looking at a powder keg. To be altogether honest, I am surprised the situation doesn't go bad more often. However, I do know why it doesn't go bad more often. The reason why is because officers tend to attempt to negate the variables. Officers are individuals, so they tend to do different things based on their experiences. For the most part, they do conform to a select few standards.

Some officers advise the driver to get out of the vehicle at every stop. They give orders over the loudspeaker. They shine that bright light at the car so the passengers can't see their location. Some officers use this practice. It is a safer practice because they can see the driver as he walks to them. They can better assess the situation. They can ask the driver who's all in the car. They don't have to approach a vehicle with tinted windows, not knowing if someone is pointing a weapon at them. Also, if the occasion calls for it, they can put the driver in between themselves and the vehicle. It's a gamble assuming the passengers harbor no ill will toward the driver. It's a good bet they like the driver more than they dislike the officer. If an officer has ever approached a vehicle only to realize its full of people when he got there, he may have decided this is the best way.

If an officer is in a more political place, you know the ones, he may not use this practice. The officer may prefer to leave all of his violators in the car so he can approach the vehicle. He may want to see who is in the vehicle. He may want to smell the car (that's right, smell the car)! He may want to see the driver and the passenger and how they react to him. There is also the possibility that the person cannot get out of the car. Perhaps they are disabled. Perhaps they are someone's grandmother who can't stand for an extended period. If an officer has had an encounter or two of this kind, perhaps now he approaches the vehicle. The fact that he approaches the vehicle does not say that the dangers that he endures while approaching the vehicle have lessened, only that he endures them. This is the way of the police officer. He endures what others do not.

I once had a vehicle run a red light. I remember it well. It was a small, black, older-model, pickup truck. I made a quick U-turn and got after the vehicle. I turned on my lights. The vehicle traveled on for a couple blocks, not even slowing down. I hit the siren. The vehicle did not miss a beat. I could not see what the driver was doing, as he had a bunch of junk in his window, but it seemed to me, he was refusing to stop. I called the stop in and advised the driver was refusing to stop. To me, the odd part about this whole situation was that the driver was not currently speeding, and he was obeying the traffic rules. He just wasn't stopping. After at least ten blocks, I was starting to get frustrated. I was whaling the siren to no avail. I pulled alongside the vehicle and yelled at the guy, "Pull over!" As he started to slow, I quickly positioned my vehicle in front of his so that he could not take off again. I jumped out of my unit weapon drawn. I approached this driver in full felony stop position yelling at him, "GET OUT OF THE TRUCK!"

I noticed he was reaching in the glove compartment as if I was saying nothing. Because he was not looking at me at the moment, I quickly repositioned myself to be on his left side as opposed to being nearly in front of the vehicle. That way, if he did raise up with a weapon in his hand and start firing, I wouldn't be where he last saw me. When the man did finally raise up, I saw that he had a notepad and pencil. Upon getting him out of the vehicle and a quick Terry frisk for weapons, I found out the problem. There was a breakdown in communication. He was deaf. That, of course, didn't negate the fact that he had run the light like anyone else. I had never previously, or since then, dealt with another deaf person. However, I did learn the lesson well, and I treat every stop as if there is a surprise ending.

The tactics I use on a traffic stop are designed to mitigate the danger I'm in while performing my duties. I have no wish to minimize your worth or make you feel uncomfortable.

22

Big Ass Gun

When I was a young person, I was very homophobic. I was never around people who were gay, nor did I know much about the culture. As a part of this ignorance, my friends and I constantly made jokes about being gay—not necessarily about us being gay but taking actions that would cause other people to think you were gay. Among my equally immature friends, you could barely do anything without being accused of being gay.

I'm a grown-up now. I have learned more about people. I now feel like if it makes you happy and does not hurt me, then more power to you. I do still suffer from some of the drawbacks of that childlike mindset, especially when it comes to searching someone. That is a true invasion of privacy and personal space. I am not a fan of touching someone's junk. Men, in general, don't like touching each other. When I was a teenager, we often joked about the lack of close contact between men. We mocked and made fun of any close contact, saying, "That's gay." I have grown up a bit since then. Even so, I still don't enjoy touching dudes. When I first started in the department, I found it difficult to search people: for females, because I didn't want to be that guy to get accused of sexual harassment, for males because…you know, they are dudes. I had no problem checking all the usual places but people don't tend to stick to the script. I knew the importance of it. I simply didn't search thoroughly enough. Who wants to grab a guy's bum? Who wants to search a guy's crotch? I can tell you, I am truly opposed to it.

To arrest people means you are taking away their freedom. Freedom is one of the most important things that any person has. That is to say, the possibility of an arrest makes people desperate. Desperation makes for strange behavior.

I no longer have problems with searching people. I don't care if you are a woman, man—or in today's world—a position in the middle. If I arrest you, or even have you in my custody, you get a thorough search free of charge.

I remember well what changed my mind. I was patrolling one of my favorite neighborhoods when I noticed a gentleman who I had reason to suspect was guilty of a crime. For the life of me, I can't remember what the charge was. I don't remember what the probable cause was for me to approach him. I remember that I had a short foot pursuit. It was really quick. I was able to keep the young man in sight for the entire duration of the foot pursuit. When I caught up with him, I had to wrestle him for a moment, but he gave up pretty quickly. I was able to safely get the cuffs on him, which is usually when someone who is holding something will fight the hardest. This young man gave up without much of a fuss. When I went for a quick search, there was no issue even then.

I searched his pant legs. I searched his pockets. I searched his waistband with no results. When I searched his crotch area, he was calm for a moment, then resisted. In retrospect, that should have been a heads up. Since he resisted, I searched better. I still didn't find anything. I felt like there was an issue, but I did not find anything. As I placed him in the car, he calmed down a bit. I assumed he had dope on his person somewhere. I knew it had to be in a place I couldn't search on the street. Like a lot of police, I use this trick to get to those hidden treasures. We will place a suspect in the backseat with whatever he has hidden that we can't find. The suspect inevitably hides whatever he was in the seats. We tend to be okay with this method because we have usually done a pretty good search and not found a weapon. If we could not find anything, it is likely because the item was small, a drug or something of the like. The suspect is cuffed, so the officer feels pretty safe.

As we rode back to the district, I watched him. He squirmed and wiggled. As he saw me watch him, he steadied. He would move, then see me see him. He would then tighten up. I watched him closely. I watched him so closely that I was certain that he had been unable to slip anything in the seats. I was disappointed, to say the least. I knew I should perhaps look away longer to give him the time he needed to get the item out. However, I was nervous due to his initial reaction when I searched him. We made it to the district in short order. As I got out of the unit and made my way to the rear passenger door, I saw that he was able to get something out. He had a shiny .357 on the floorboard. For anyone who has seen this weapon, it's a very large revolver. To this day, I don't know where he could have hidden that weapon. I don't care what the scenario is now. I do a thorough search. If that makes you uncomfortable, I truly understand, and I'm not sorry.

23

Hit and Run, Suspect and the Victim

Everyone loves a car pursuit. Police like them as much as the guy on the couch watching them does, even more so. The thrill of moving so fast is…a thrill. Any opportunity to get into one, I would likely take it. Of course, there is a downside. Any damage that I do or cause while chasing someone is my fault. Obviously, if I run over a pedestrian, there will be consequences. What's not so obvious is any damage done by the bad guy is, get this, also my fault. If someone dies when the bad guy runs stop signs and red lights while I'm in pursuit, it's the officer's fault. That being said, most officers avoid pursuits and the liability that comes with them. As a rookie, I wouldn't pass one up. As a more seasoned officer, I will definitely pass. Often, even before the officer can decide the chase is too dangerous, the supervisor will step in to cancel it. The supervisor will weigh the charges and see if the pursuit is worth the risk. If they deem the risk not worthy, they will supersede the officer and call the pursuit off. That's right, they will let the bad guy go! If the bad guy goes out and commits another crime, that's a tragedy. If he runs over someone while being pursued by you, that's a tragedy and a lawsuit. There was a time when I had the opportunity to engage in a pursuit that I could not have been held liable for (the best kind). This, this right here, is the reason to go into law enforcement, besides all the noble stuff.

I'm patrolling my usual neighborhood when I hear over the radio that my supervisor is behind a vehicle that is refusing to stop. This scenario is great because a superior is involved. Not only is he involved, but he is also the initiator of the chase. That means he is unlikely to call it off, and he holds primary responsibility for any damage that may be incurred.

Ladies and gentlemen, this is the stuff of legends. This is the perfect storm. All of the television high-speed pursuits I've watched have prepared me for this.

That being said, I jumped right in behind his unit. The pursuit lasted about four blocks and never got any speed. The driver turned a couple of corners and then pulled into a parking lot—anticlimactic, I know. The driver jumped out of the car so fast that he was unable to put the SUV he was driving into park. He attempted to jump out of the vehicle and run into an apartment complex door opening. It was a brick wall with an opening in the shape of an arch. Ironically enough, my supervisor and I pulled up immediately as he jumped out of the vehicle, just in time to see the SUV keep rolling forward. As the suspect jumped out of the SUV and rushed toward the entrance, he didn't quite make it. He was caught in between the car and the wall next to the entrance to the complex. He literally ran over himself. As I saw this, I paused to wince. In this mere moment I wasted, the vehicle rolled back off his legs. I assumed that he would collapse in pain from what was clearly a very serious situation. Surprisingly, the suspect simply took off running. This is where the supervisor leading the vehicle pursuit turns into a less motivating situation. Supervisors tend to be older. In this particular scenario, the supervisor was quite a few pounds heavier. Bottom line, the supervisor was not going after him on foot.

"Get him!" were the only words the supervisor stated. A two to three-second head start is a lifetime in a foot pursuit. I almost immediately snapped out of my amazed state, resulting from the invulnerable suspect, to get after him. I chased him across an open parking lot and then a courtyard of a large apartment complex. Combined, the complex parking lot and the courtyard were about the length of a football field. At a full sprint carrying the standard gear of the time (approximately twenty-five pounds), it was hard. It would have been easier if I had gained some yardage on the suspect. I did not. I maintained a solid four-yard distance from him the entire length of the chase. Four yards is close enough to motivate me to keep going but too far to dive after him.

The courtyard was not empty, not by a long shot. People were sitting on cars and children running around. There were groups of teenagers standing around shoo shooing and entertaining themselves. Not anymore. The suspect and I were now the main event, and this was an interactive event. There were chants, "You ain't gonna catch him. You ain't gonna catch him!" I wish I could say these chants were beneath me. I wish I could say that I am in no way affected by my environment. I wish I could say that no matter what is said, I maintain my composure and professional behavior. Unfortunately, this is not so. I responded, "Shiiiiiiddd, I bet I catch him!" Side note, it is expected of the police to yell out loud, clear commands of what you expect the suspect to do. We have to be clear so that there is no misunderstanding of what we expect from a suspect who is, ideally, supposed to be following our commands. In that regard, I started by yelling, "Stop!" After chasing the suspect for about 100 to 150 yards, my commands changed to, "You might as well give up. I got you. You know you tired! They know you ain't getting away." The children and teenagers and adults were now totally engaged in the foot pursuit. We were the afternoon's entertainment.

The suspect eventually closed in on one particular apartment building. The building was a two-floor, compound-type building.

There was one entrance in the front placed at the center of the building. Once you enter the main entrance, there was a courtyard. Once inside, you could see a row of apartments lined along both sides of the walkways to the right and the left. There were six apartment doors on your right side, which were mirrored on the left side. You could see the three apartments on the right and left. There were also two doors that were hidden in an alleyway that disappeared under stairwells on either side. This same pattern was repeated upstairs on both sides. Directly in front of you, about a quarter of the distance from the back of the compound, was a single apartment door. A copy of that door was upstairs as well. To the right and to the left, the two alleyways led to the parking lot. The suspect ran around the entire compound, and so did I.

At this point, I was exhausted. Luckily, so was the suspect. We were a slow-moving spectacle. He was maintaining a three-yard lead on me as I jogged behind him. I was visually tired. I was also calling the foot pursuit on the radio. I was still dealing with the mocking of my cheering and jeering crowd. I knew these people. They knew me. I would speak with a lot of them on the regular. This was my neighborhood. It was not only the neighborhood I worked in; it was also the neighborhood I grew up in. I recognized a lot of the faces. However, I was focused on my bad guy as he made his second lap around the building. I had not gained a foot in closing the distance between the suspect and myself. I could say for certain that we were both exhausted. I can't say for certain, but I suspect that people could have walked faster than we were running. The suspect was pouring sweat. I could see him clear as day. I was certain that he would give up at any moment. One moment led to the next and continued to stretch into the next. "Stop dammit!" I wanted to give up, but I could not. I would not. In front of this crowd, that would motivate the next person to simply run until I was tired.

I was not a track star. I was also at a disadvantage being I had to carry all of this extra gear. Still, I continued after the suspect, maintaining a close pursuit at an impractical, slow pace. After the suspect made his third revolution around the compound, I had gotten no closer, but nor had I gotten any farther away. About halfway through the fourth revolution, the suspect chose to enter the compound as opposed to going around. I was unmoved by this change of venue because there was still an exit at the back of the compound, two alleyways that led back to where we had just come. This was not a fatal error made by the suspect.

The suspect entered the compound, and instead of going straight through to the exit, he chose to enter the left stairwell. Finally! He has made the mistake that would allow me to stop this endless pursuit. I followed the suspect up the stairs and to the end of a short hall/alleyway. The hall ended in an opening closed in by a waist-high gate, which kept people from falling over. However, the suspect was not prepared to give up his escape. Without a moment's hesitation, he jumped over the rail. As he went down, he grabbed onto the rail to slow his fall. Unfortunately…for him, he did not get a good grip and only threw his landing into disarray. I saw that he hit the ground, which was unforgiving concrete, hard. The suspect hit the ground first with his feet then caught his forward momentum with his hands. The momentum seemed to be too much for his hands to absorb, so his face and chest took the rest of it. I was in such "hot pursuit" that my adrenaline pushed my right foot to the top of the gate before my mind caught up and yelled at me STOP! With a deep disgusted breath, I turned around to run back down the stairs with just a candlelight of hope that my suspect would still be in sight by the time I reached his landing site. After I reached the bottom of the stairs and turned the corner to go to the bottom path where the suspect should have gone, I heard the crowd, and I saw the suspect. It appeared he was hurt. As I approached, still exhausted, he jumped up and began to run again. @$%$*^$$#^*^^%#^&%$@#! I can't express my dissatisfaction with the fact that this pursuit was not yet over. I could see that the suspect was a bit different now. His stride did not look quite as graceful as it had previously. His arms were both curled up to his chest, reminiscent of chicken wings. He was running forward but canted to his left side so that it appeared he was running sideways. There was one more thing I had noticed. I was not closer. Being that I had very little left in my reserves, I decided to go for it. I turned up the speed and dove on the suspect. He went down easily. He screamed in agony. I could barely hear him over my own heartbeat. He was tired. Anyone could see this. However, I know that the most dangerous time that a suspect and a police officer share is when the cuffs are being put on. The suspect knows that often this is his last taste of freedom, at least for a time. This is usually when they get their burst of energy to fight. I was careful. I was able to cuff him without incident. Then, I collapsed. The suspect was lying face down with his hands behind his back while I was lying horizontal to him using his back as my pillow. Truly, I could not move if I had to. It was a scary moment for me. I was counting on the fact that any minute my backup would arrive. I also knew that the ever-present crowd was not my friend. I had been so gracious as to be their entertainment for the evening, but I knew that I was still in danger while they were there. Then, I heard what could only be labeled applause. Mission accomplished.

After backup arrived and I caught my breath for the long walk back to my unit, we realized the suspect was injured. EMS was contacted. When we get back to the suspect's vehicle, we found a gun, cocaine and a child. My supervisor who stayed with the vehicle was now a babysitter and he had to stay with the car lest the bad guy circle the block and drive away. Fortunately, when back up arrived, he sent them in my direction. As we processed the vehicle on scene, EMS arrived. We found that during the suspect's death-defying leap—that I almost repeated—he broke both his wrists. The suspect also fractured a bone in his leg. The suspect had to be transported to the hospital. While I was extremely satisfied with the outcome of this foot pursuit, I was not happy that the suspect was injured. I know this makes me seem altruistic, but that is not the case. When a suspect is injured during an arrest, the arresting officer has to sit at the hospital and guard the suspect while he is being treated. I don't know if you've ever been in a hospital before, but they are crowded. That, coupled with the fact that the process takes a long time, makes for an unhappy officer.

After sitting in the hospital with the suspect for five hours, he had multiple casts. It turns out the guy was a cool person save for the guns, the drugs and the irresponsible parenting.

24

We Don't Recognize You

A long while or so after this encounter, I was in Walmart with my family when a male approached me. He seemed really familiar, but I was certain I didn't know him. He walked up and said, "Hey, man, how you been?" Since he had started talking without introducing himself, I assumed I was supposed to know him. I continued on, "I'm doing fine. How 'bout yourself?" After a short discussion about who knows what, my son asked me who this person was. This was not unexpected because I teach my son to introduce himself and shake a person's hand. Until this moment, I had been frantically going through my memory in an effort to recall from where I knew this person. My time had run out. "I don't know, son; he didn't introduce himself." The guy had a sly grin, as he had likely realized a lot sooner that I didn't know who he was. He promptly brought his hands up close to his stomach below his chest in a chicken-wing pose. He placed emphasis on his wrists, which were both broken the last time we met.

The guy explained how he had not been in any trouble since that incident and how he appreciated me being kind while he was in the hospital.

I make it my business to be nice, or at least respectful to everyone because you never know when you will see them again.

25

Rich Boy Bad Guy Preferential Treatment

Officers know there are differences in the treatment of criminals based on their economic status. One could most certainly argue there are other differences based on color, creed, religion or other caveat, but with finance there is no discussion. If a person has money, there are doors forced open, whereas, for the destitute, phone calls are ignored. What a lot of people don't know is that the preferential treatment often is created at a much higher level than the street officer. The treatment is often higher than the detective level. Most often, police want to see justice served as much as you. We want to see the bad guy go to jail. If the bad guy is free because of some simple loophole, its bad. If a bad guy goes free because of a mistake we made, that's worse. If a bad guy is free just because he has enough money to pay the right people, we are just as disgusted as you are. I can't say for certain that every officer has had to deal with these problems, but I have.

I received a call at about 1:30 in the morning advising there was a victim suffering from a knife wound to the shoulder. The victim would be transported to the hospital with non-life-threatening injuries. The on-scene sergeant advised that the victim did not, or would not, say who had stabbed her.

The call was not from the usual place where these kinds of calls usually originated. This call came from City Place. This was one of the wealthiest neighborhoods in the city. There were armed security guards at the entrance to the neighborhood. The entire neighborhood was fenced off. The neighborhood was huge. The homes were immense and elegant. The yards were all manicured, and there were two helicopter pads near the golf course. For me, this was a treat. I hadn't been to this area before. I was not allowed. If you did not know anyone in the area, the guards would not allow you entry. As far as I knew, there were no police patrols in this neighborhood. Still, when someone gets stabbed, and EMS is called, they want to make sure the scene is safe, so the police are called with EMS. They know for a fact someone is stabbing people in that area.

Because I was already out in the field, I arrived on scene fairly quickly. I arrived in time to see the victim, a female, being put in an ambulance with seven inches of knife (five additional inches of handle) sticking out of her shoulder. The victim seemed to be calm, so I asked her what had happened. Before she was wheeled off, she advised it was an accident. There were two other people in the residence, a fifteen-year-old boy and a man who was about the age of the victim. I would assume that he was the husband. Upon speaking to the man, he said that he had just arrived home and had not seen what happened. He could not provide any useful information. However, I could see that he was visibly upset with the fifteen-year-old. Upon speaking with the fifteen-year-old, he began to cry but would not say anything. I was even cut short by the man who advised he was the father and did not give his permission to speak with the child. I explained to him that I did not need his permission and that this was an active investigation.

Side note on juveniles, you are allowed to speak with juveniles as witnesses or victims without their parents' present. However, you are not allowed to speak to them without their parents present if they are the suspects. Considering the response of the parents, the mother's casual stab victim demeanor and the father's rising hostility, I was starting to think that perhaps the fifteen-year-old may, in fact, be the suspect. From what physical evidence I had on scene, there appeared to have been a struggle, but there appeared to be no sign of forced entry. The kitchen had a couple broken dishes and a few things that may or may not have been out of place. However, the mother did say it was an accident. After the scene was photographed, I went to the hospital to speak with the mother in an effort to get more information. I suspected the fifteen-year-old was going to be the suspect, but you can't accuse someone of stabbing their mother just because you have a hunch. I left an officer on the scene with the father, just in case, to keep an eye on the father and son.

Upon speaking to the mother, she advised she was working in the kitchen when she slipped and fell on the knife. This was clearly a made-up story. Side note: Police are allowed to lie. I told her the doctor said the angle of entry meant the knife could not be self-inflicted. How could she know otherwise? I also told her, her husband said her son had been having some problems and that he thought something like this might happen. The mother immediately burst into tears, yelling, "He didn't mean it," and "It was my fault." She and the fifteen-year-old had been having an argument. The argument was about having the cleaning crew clean his house when they cleaned the main house. This fifteen-year-old kid lived in the pool house. This simple argument erupted into the juvenile stabbing five inches of a seven-inch blade into his mother's shoulder. This was all I needed to hear.

Before we go too far off-topic, understand that I realize the kid needs help. I would like you to understand, that's not my job. It is not my function to correct this behavior or give therapy. I do, on occasion, verbally correct dysfunctional behavior. I may even give therapy from time to time. However, when a crime is perpetrated, my first duty is to protect the populace and to place the perpetrator in jail.

I contacted the officer and told him to place the fifteen-year-old under arrest. I was immediately told that the fifteen-year-old was no longer on scene. I was told that he had been transferred to a medical facility for a twenty-four-hour hold. I was told by powers higher than myself that I was to leave him in the facility and that if I was going to arrest him, then to arrest him when he was released. FINE! I was advised by the facility manager that the juvenile would be released the following morning at 10:00 am. I must admit I was a bit upset with these events.

A detective is in charge of a scene once he arrives and takes it over. All of the uniformed officers are under the authority of that detective. While a captain or major or chief technically outranks the detective, in theory, when it comes to the case, the detective is where the buck stops. If there is any interference, there has to be a reason because it could hinder the case.

This is why this is such a strange situation. I had told the officer to keep watch on the father and son. This meant they do not get to leave. Even if they were somehow allowed to leave, I was to be notified. I was not notified. The officer I posted was relieved by his supervisor.

I was at the facility with my paperwork complete at 5:00 am. I asked if the juvenile was going to be released, and they said he would be released at 8:00 am. I had originally been told 10:00 am. While I waited in the parking lot until 8:00 am, I was advised that the juvenile would be held for further observation. When I questioned when he would be released, I was advised that, at this time, it was unknown. I started making calls to supervisors and supervisors' supervisors. I was being told that I could not arrest him until he was released. I was upset, to say the least. This was not what I would have been told for someone who lived in Dalton Estates. I was being told that since he was a juvenile, I could not interfere with his medical treatment. They were treating this case as if he had a genuine medical issue and he was being treated medically. FINE! Without telling anyone involved in the case, I immediately went back to my office and drew up a juvenile arrest warrant for the fifteen-year-old. I had the juvenile warrant signed by a supervisor who was not my own. I then took the juvenile warrant to the judge. The judge found probable cause to arrest the juvenile and so he signed the warrant. As per our procedure, I then took the warrant to be filed into the clerk of courts. The warrant was then placed into our database. The final step before being placed into the database is a once over by the people who place the warrant in the system. If there is any problem with the warrant, they reject it. Then, you have to recall the warrant. That is to say, you have to explain to the judge that you made a mistake, fix it and get another warrant signed. No one wants to do that. You appear to be an incompetent detective when you have to do that. The juvenile warrant was accepted without incident.

I went back to the facility and explained to them that there was an active warrant for the arrest of the juvenile. I explained to them in no uncertain terms that they were to call the police before he was released. The responding officer would place the juvenile under arrest. Problem solved.

Seven days go by, and I have not received word that the juvenile has been released. I have called twice in seven days, and both times, I was advised that he was still there, and they had no idea when he would be released. On the seventh day, I received a call from the data unit. They advised that I was missing a social security number on the warrant, and it would need to be recalled. I have written quite a few juvenile warrants, and I have never had a social security number on them. The social security number for a juvenile was often difficult to get being the parents rarely wanted to help, and juveniles aren't in a lot of databases. I explained this in detail. I had them pull up other juvenile warrants I'd written to see that they had been accepted without social security numbers. They were insistent that I would have to recall this warrant.

I have never had a warrant in the system for over a week before it was decided the warrant needed to be recalled. I know that it is futile to argue with the data people. If they decide you have to recall the warrant, then that's it. You have to recall it. FINE! I recalled the warrant. It took two hours, and that was extremely fast considering the process. By the time I placed the warrant back in the system and called the facility to check his status, I was advised that he had been released from that facility and that he had been transferred to another facility in Utah.

It was clear to me that someone had pulled some strings here to keep Mr. Affluenza free. I placed the warrant into the database anyway. I was pretty certain wherever he was, this case would be cleared up without him doing any jail time. Anyone who reads this, I assure you I am just as upset about this injustice as you are.

Please understand, even now, I have no personal grudge with this kid. I understand his parents doing everything they can to ensure their child is taken care of. I would likely do the same for my kid. My problem is the people in the department and in the local government, allowing this to occur. This is not a unique event. I have arrested plenty of juveniles who have hurt their parents. I've dealt with plenty of parents who, even after the juvenile has injured them, will defend the juvenile to the end. I've seen those parents fail time and time again. In most cases, the juvenile was charged and eventually got the help he needed. Most times, these events occur in poor households. These parents don't have the resources available to these people. That is unfair, and the law should be equal for all.

26

Fight on Jackson Street

Law enforcement is an exciting job. There is something new to do every day. One day you can have a day filled with traffic tickets. The next day you could be involved in a shooting. The two drastically different days could also be the same day. Every day that you spend in this job should—I reiterate—should be like your first day. You should be extremely cautious. You should take a lesson in every event. You should approach every situation by the book with every precaution.

One cold, cold night, I received a call. The victim, a twenty-two-year-old female, advised her ex-boyfriend was stalking her. I was advised the victim stated the suspect had been to her residence multiple times that particular night.

When I pulled up on scene, I scanned the area. I parked in front of the residence next door. There were two cars in the driveway, one blue and one purple. Both cars belonged to the residence. The suspect was supposed to drive a blue 1980 Cutlass. The coast was clear. I didn't see the suspect, but to be super safe, I advised dispatch to let the victim know I was on scene, and I circled the house on foot just to check the backyard. There were no signs of the suspect. I walked up on the porch and knocked on the door. The victim came to the door and advised the suspect had been back to the residence numerous times that day. She advised her "boyfriend" was a drug dealer. She said, somehow, and for some unknown reason, he decided to try his own product. The ex-boyfriend was now a bothersome crackhead who was constantly borrowing money and stealing items from the residence. I asked the victim, "When was the last time you saw him?" She said, "Now." As I paused to follow her gaze, my heart jumped from average resting heartrate to PREPARE FOR BATTLE!

We looked into the purple car and saw this fool lying down in the driver seat. I had looked in the window as I passed, but due to the dark windows, I hadn't been able to make out a person hiding. I had even pulled the door handle to see if it was locked. But of course, from the vantage point of the porch and the absence of tint on the front windshield, I could make out the suspect quite well. I advised dispatch I needed another unit out to my location. Unfortunately, due to the nature of things, when I saw him, he saw me seeing him. I jumped off the porch in an effort to catch him, and he quickly jumped out of the driver-side door and stood up to see me on the passenger side. I ran toward the back of the vehicle, so he ran to the front. I stopped and changed directions, and so did he. After a short while, I saw how this was going. I ducked down so he couldn't see me and run to the rear of the car. As I suspected, he tried to run to the rear of the car, and I tackled him. It was at this moment that I noticed how much larger this "crackhead" was than I was. It was too late. I had to fight this guy.

Let me take a moment to acknowledge why criminals have the advantage in a fistfight with police. Police have to fight with the intention of apprehending the suspect. Our goal is to restrain the suspect. No matter how much energy is expended during the confrontation, that should be my goal. On the other hand, the suspect's agenda could vary widely. His intention could be to escape. It could be to beat me to a pulp. It could be to kill me. It could be as simple as to get in a few good licks before he decides to give up.

So, I engaged this guy. I was fighting to get ahold of his hand so that I could get the cuffs on. He was trying to get away. I grabbed ahold of the sweater he was wearing, and he quickly came out of it and ran. Oddly enough, he had no undershirt on. So, I was chasing this shirtless crackhead in the dark. I was in a foot pursuit. Foot pursuits are fun, most of the time. As previously stated, as a rookie, I enjoyed the excitement of the chase. In this particular scenario, I had already engaged the suspect before the foot pursuit even began. That means my energy reserves were already on the way down.

One of the hardest things about a foot pursuit is letting help know where you are. You have to tell help that you are headed west on Jackson Street. You have to give landmarks. You also have to catch up with the suspect. Just remember, which way is west is difficult when under stress. If the suspect is constantly changing directions, it can feel impossible. I eventually chased the suspect behind a building somewhere on Jackson Street. I assumed he realized he couldn't shake me. He then decided to fight. Keep in mind that this was a few years back, and we did not have Tasers. I would have been much better off with a Taser. Instead, I had to fight this person on uneven ground in the dark while still trying to alert help where I was. The fight felt like it went on forever. I was really tired and pretty certain this guy wasn't as tired as I was.

It's at this time you remember how police are at a severe disadvantage in a fight.

As I fought with this larger opponent, I realized that I had moved beyond the ability to draw my weapon because I wouldn't have the energy to retain it. It's at this moment I saw a police car pass by. They didn't see us. I yelled into the radio, "You just passed me!" In my mind, I gave a calm statement that said exactly what I wanted to convey. The statement was made specifically to the officer who passed me as sure as if I had said it directly to his face. In reality, I had yelled, "You passed me," on the radio. The statement was yelled at every officer who was listening to the radio including all the officers rushing to my aid. I could hear the screeching of the tires as multiple cars slammed on breaks. In what seemed like a very long time, my assistance came. They took the suspect into custody very quickly. All was well again.

This case turned out well. I survived what could have been a really bad situation. The truth of the matter is, it could have been a lot worse than it turned out. I could have easily been shot or stabbed. I had missed the suspect, but I was certain he didn't miss me. I'm sure he had seen my unit when it arrived. He had seen me walk around the car and step on the porch. If he had decided to shoot me, he would have had a few shots before I would even realize the direction the bullets came from. I'd chased this suspect into a dark backyard. I didn't know if he had any weapons on him. I knew he was high. I should have kept in contact with dispatch. The victim should have let me know that he had returned. I shouldn't have gotten out without backup, though it's usually not available. I made a lot of mistakes, and out of sheer luck, I'm alive and can have a chance to do better in the future.

27

Shit Happens, Even to Me

Putting on a persona all day is difficult. Like I said, its like flexing a muscle. You may be able to hold it for a while, but eventually you are going to have to relax. If you hold it too long that muscle starts to twitch. At some jobs, as long as you have their uniform on, you are expected to behave in a certain manor because you represent the company. However, when you take the uniform off, you are free to be you. That is not the case as a police officer. If something bad happens, you are the police, uniformed or not. There is no relief for that muscle.

Officers understand that things sometimes happen. Things can get out of control at any time. All we can do as upstanding citizens is try to minimize these encounters by taking preventative steps. If you know a place is dangerous or boisterous, avoid it. If you know people are violent or troublemakers, avoid them. Sometimes, no matter what you do, there isn't anything you can do to avoid the trouble that finds you.

Dre and I have been friends since middle school. We both grew up in Dalton Estates and lived a couple of doors down from each other. We have different personalities and different statures. I am, or at least I consider myself, a tough guy. Dre does not. He considers himself a lover not a fighter. Dre is an architect. He draws up plans for building construction. He is a professional and carries himself as such. Dre carries a firearm, which is his right. He carries his firearm in his vehicle at all times. As I have said, Dre is not a fighter and has no intention of engaging in fisticuffs. Neither does he plan to allow himself to be hurt if he can avoid it.

I was out with Dre on a much needed off day. Dre and I went to a bar that was nice but was for an older crowd. At the time, Dre and I were both young. I was about twenty-four and he about twenty-two. We were single. We were both professionals with hard jobs. We went out together because we had a similar mindset. We grew up in a rough neighborhood. Neither of us had criminal records because we avoided foolishness as best we could. We avoided the people in the neighborhood who were problems. Even though our friends were not criminals, they made bad decisions. They got into fights with kids from other neighborhoods. Dre and I avoided these scenarios whenever we could. A little bit of luck and we made it through adolescence unscathed. These friends continued their bad decision making into adulthood. As an adult, the stakes were higher so we avoided these people whenever we could. Dre and I went out alone and we avoided the spots where we knew we would run into them.

When Dre and I went out, we went to talk, drink and mess with women. There were no better reasons to be out. One night, Dre and I were out having a good time—two single young professional men at a bar. The bar was full of women and so we drank and were merry. I met a nice-looking lady and asked her to dance. After multiple dances, I met Dre back at the bar. Dre had met up with a friend who he introduced me to. Dre seemed to know everyone, so this was not the first time this had happened. I sat at the bar speaking with Dre and his friend, Brett. Brett seemed like a nice enough guy. In between dances, I would come back and talk with Dre and Brett for a couple of hours. I'd gotten the number of the lady I'd been dancing with and we had seemed to hit it off. All in all, it was a good night. When the lights began to come on in the bar that meant it was time to call it a night. I had spoken with the lady and she told me she was there with some of her girlfriends who were about to go to a waffle house. I went to convince Dre to make the waffle house our next stop.

Leaving the bar en route to the car, I noticed Brett had walked with us. Perhaps he needed a ride home. Dre was driving and I was the passenger. Dre knew him so they must have discussed this while I was dancing. Brett was standing at the rear of Dre's vehicle while I was standing in the doorway on the passenger side. Dre was in the doorway on the driver's side. That was when the night went downhill rapidly.

We had just walked to the car and were about to leave when Brett realized he dropped something during the walk from the bar exit to the car. A quick look back confirmed it. Not five yards away from us, we saw what Brett dropped. It was a gallon-sized Ziplock bag of what could only be marijuana. Now, I was thinking, *THE WHOLE TIME!* The whole time we were in the bar, you had an elephant-sized bag of weed on you. I couldn't say whether Brett was selling the drug at the bar or if he'd bought it there. I looked over at Dre, who appeared as pissed as I was. Brett immediately went from standing to a quick trot to grab the bag.

The car was parked facing the wall of a building that was next to the bar. There was a car on either side of the vehicle. To leave, we had to back out and navigate our way to the exit. At this point, I was more than happy to get on my way and leave Brett standing alone in the parking lot.

Brett tried to grab the bag but just before he could, another male grabbed his dropped contraband. Brett yelled, "Hey that's me!" Without a moment's pause, the male drew a handgun and pointed it at Brett. Brett was standing just in front of a blocked in

Dre and I. Dre's weapon was in the car just under the drivers' seat. I'm an officer. I always carry a weapon but weapons aren't allowed in bars. My weapon was in the car under the front seat less than arm's reach from where I was standing.

There we were, two professionals standing in a parking lot with a drug dealer and a thief. The thief had just drawn a weapon and pointed it at "us." Dre and I were of the same mind and immediately drew our weapons. Now, Dre and I, barely able to keep pace with the rapidly changing events, stood with weapons aimed at the thief. Now, we were in a Mexican standoff over a huge bag of weed. Neither Dre nor I participate in any kind of illegal activity. Yet, somehow, I was there in the middle of this… mess! I immediately started sobering up to yell something to the effect of, "Everybody calm down!" I didn't give a shit about that weed; just let me get out of there. Brett was still standing there without a weapon, indignant, as if he was bulletproof. The thief had not lowered his weapon and didn't look like he was going to back down.

This was not going to be good. I was about to get shot outside a bar in between these cars, unable to move forward because the thief would think I was a threat, and unable to move back because of a wall. The story would read "Dirty Cop Killed in Apparent Drug Deal Gone Bad." It was at this moment the girl I'd been dancing with all evening stepped in between us. She gave me a hug and put herself between the thief and myself. The girl was the thief's sister. The thief slowly lowered his weapon. She then turned and walked toward her brother and pushed him away from Dre's vehicle. I didn't know what happened to the bag of marijuana or to Brett. Dre and I immediately got in the car and left the area and that night behind.

28

Courting the Wife

Police are police all the time. Yes, the police officer knows this, but so do the people he cares about. His family, friends, children and associates all are constantly aware of the fact he is a police officer. It's not easy to be a family member of a police officer, but there are perceived perks. Your children think you are a superhero who can take on all comers. Your wife thinks you are the authority to everyone but her. The public thinks you are someone who has elite training in a plethora of fields that make you an expert…in everything. None of these important people understands the fact that being a police officer is a calling, and there is a gratification there…for you. Beyond my personal feelings, and as far as the world is concerned, it's a job. The thing about a job is, sometimes, you have to be off duty. Sometimes, it's hard for the family and friends to grasp this concept of being off duty. Even the public thinks an officer is always on duty. Imagine if you were in a bank robbery, and you knew for a fact the person in front of you was a police officer—not in uniform mind you, just "off duty."

Before my beautiful wife gave birth to my first son, we were nervous. I was going to be a father, and I wanted to be there. In the last days before the actual date, I was afraid to leave her alone. This was her first child as well, so she was afraid to be alone. We were so close to the day; I had already taken off on paternity leave. (That's right; it's a thing.)

Even though I was off, I had a subpoena for court. I had to be in court that morning. It was important I attend because the judges like to place warrants out for your arrest if you don't show. I didn't have to be in uniform; so, I just wore slacks, a tie, and dress shoes. As I said, I didn't want to leave my wife alone, so I brought her. I also thought she could see some of the stuff I deal with at work.

The judge placed the court on a recess, so my wife and I were sitting in the front of the courthouse. We were sitting and talking when we noticed two people arguing. One was clearly a lawyer, in a semi-fine suit, glasses and a small black leather suitcase. The other man was slender, in exercise clothes, shorts and a t-shirt. The lawyer had a calm demeanor as he spoke with the other man. The other man had a thick accent. He was an African man who was clearly very upset. The argument continued for a moment before the African man escalated the argument to physical violence. The African man slapped the lawyer with such force that his glasses flew from his face landing some ten feet away. The clap sounded off, catching everyone's attention.

We had just witnessed a crime. It was not my first. For me, it wasn't even that big a deal. Who among us has not wanted to slap a lawyer at one point or another? Even so, it was just a misdemeanor, simple battery. However, my wife was shocked and frantic. You would have thought she had just witnessed a murder.

It was at this point the African man started to look around and walked away. My wife started yelling, "J, get him! Get him!" So, he started running. However, I was not prepared to engage a suspect. I was looking around for an officer on duty to handle the incident. Unfortunately, there was only one officer in earshot. This particular officer was a lieutenant, a large one. It was clear to anyone watching, this officer was not about to chase the suspect.

With my wife still yelling, "Get him," I allowed my drive to impress my wife to overwhelm my common sense. I found myself chasing a slender African man down the street for a misdemeanor, in dress shoes. I am not a track star, and the irony of chasing a slender African man in athletic gear was not lost on me.

While in hot pursuit on foot, I realized my situation. First off, I'm in civilian clothes. Does this guy know I'm a police officer? I have on some dress shoes that were never meant to run in. There is the issue of what to do when I catch him. I don't have handcuffs. Am I supposed to wrestle this guy to the ground? What if he has a weapon? What if he decides he doesn't want to cooperate? By far, the most important thing is: What if I have to return to my new young blushing bride without this guy? I will never win an argument again.

I chase this guy about half a mile up the road before he finally gives up. Luckily, he goes down without a fight. I have to wait not less than thirty minutes before the lieutenant shows up with a pair of cuffs. The entire time I'm waiting, I'm basically sitting on this guy. We walk this guy back to the courthouse to deal with this issue.

As I arrive back at the courthouse, I see my wife there. I see all thirty-two of her teeth as she smiles so proudly at me. She is basically cheering me on. The guy whose freedom I just took sees her too.

I did a few stupid things back to back compounded on top of other stupid things just to see that smile. Police want to be heroes to their family too.

I chased a guy with no resources. I had no cuffs, no weapon, no bullet-resistant vest or Taser. What if this guy decided he was not going to jail today? Had this guy been wanted for murder, he would have likely been willing to fight me to a standstill. The moment I chased this guy could have been the last time I saw my wife, all because I wanted to be a hero.

29

The Suspect is the Victim and the Victim is the Suspect

In the movies, you see the gritty, weathered, five-day-unshaven, trench-coat-wearing detectives who are the toughest of the tough. The detectives have hearts of gold and take no prisoners. They are unstoppable workaholics whose only weakness is the things they have seen over their long careers. There is always that scene when they are in the middle of some traumatic event where their partner, friend or some innocent child was just out of reach losing their life and forever changing his. It's at this moment the detective wakes up in a cold sweat alone in his bed. The camera pans out as he reluctantly gets up and adjusts to his new state of consciousness. The watcher is able to see that he is living in a filthy house. There are dirty dishes and laundry everywhere. He grabs some old Chinese takeout and sips the last of a pint of something before heading out to take care of business and make up for that one haunting mistake.

Police see many things that would turn your stomach or make you cry. While there is plenty of help out there for the officer, he has to seek it. You have to admit you have an issue and you have to tell someone that you have taken in a bit more than you can handle. That is not likely. An officer will suffer alone because he helps people. He does not need help. The unseen injury is left to fester and grow into an open sore. It will eventually turn into something the world can see. In the meantime, it is covered by a smile.

I have always considered myself fortunate. I do not hold onto things I've seen. I am so inclined to let things go. I do remember them, in detail, but I do not hold onto them. I am not a religious man, but out of all the prayers out there my favorite is the serenity prayer. "God, grant me the serenity to accept the things that I cannot change." I love that line. If a person has been murdered, it is a terribly sad thing. However, as callous as it may sound, I have not taken a loss. My job is not to feel the pain but to ease it in others by seeking out justice for that lost soul. As of about fifteen years back, I took this prayer and way of thinking to heart. When I am working, I am merely in this world but not of it.

I don't remember all my cases. One case that I remember, I worked as the primary detective. I remember the scene well because it was a sunny, pretty day. We received a call advising a victim had been located on Jersey Street—a middle-aged man with a single gunshot wound. The victim, who had been shot one time in the head, was lying in the road in front of his home. The man was not a large man. He was about 5'9", 200 to 220 lbs. The man was wearing a blue t-shirt, black pants with a baseball cap. The man's legs were bent sharply at the knee in a way that gave the impression that he had been standing still when he fell. The man's hat, a brown baseball cap, was still on his head. His head was in a pool of blood. There was a small hole in the side of the hat. The hole had a small black halo-like ring around it slightly off center of the hole. The ring center was a little higher than the hole giving the hole the appearance of small black ball with gray smoke rising from it. The scene was documented and pictures were taken. The area was searched. Eventually, the coroner came onto the scene to collect the remains and take the gentleman away.

The reporter of this incident, an anonymous complainant, had advised there had been an argument between the victim and a female. The content of the argument was not given, only that the female had placed a gun to the man's head and fired. The female had walked away long before the police arrived. A canvass of the neighborhood found a lot of reluctant people not wanting to be involved with this serious situation. They were reluctant but the canvass did turn up a suspect. She was a thirty-year-old female who lived somewhere in the immediate vicinity. The female had been seen at the residence more than once. The people I spoke with advised the woman had a drug problem. They also advised the victim wasn't exactly a nice guy.

It wasn't long before we identified the female by name. We secured a picture and placed her in a photographic lineup. We located a few witnesses who had seen the incident and were willing to participate in the photographic lineup process. The witnesses, all, immediately and positively identified the female as the person who fired a single shot into the victim's head. She was the person who casually walked away from the scene in no particular rush after the horrendous act. The female had been arrested multiple times for possession of drug paraphernalia, entry and remaining after being forbidden, prostitution and an assortment of other minor crimes. She was never arrested for anything approaching the seriousness of this incident.

A warrant was written for the arrest of the female suspect who had been positively identified. The judge signed the warrant and a wanted poster was produced. The email was sent out to the department. Within an hour, I received a call. The female had been picked up. The officer transported her to my office so she could be interviewed. Another thirty minutes and she was in the holding cell waiting to be questioned.

She appeared exhausted and weathered. Her clothes were not

clean and her hair was in a single unkempt topknot. She had been picked up in a pink, sleeveless shirt that was too big for her. She wore pajama pants that had a red and green plaid pattern reminiscent of Christmas. You shouldn't judge a person by a single appearance but it was clear she had been through a lot. She was of small stature, no more than 5'1". She couldn't have been more than 110 pounds.

The female was read her rights per Miranda and she signed a waiver to that effect without so much as a word of resistance. The female was asked if she had been on Jersey Street that day and she advised she had been. When asked what she was doing there, she advised without much of a display of emotion, that she had shot the man. While the next question from me should have been "With what?" it wasn't. I could have asked where was the gun, but I didn't. The next question I asked was not the most pressing to the case but the most pressing on my mind. "Why?"

A confession to a murder doesn't happen every day, but it does happen. Usually, when someone commits a murder and gets caught, the last thing they want to do is cop to it. If they wanted to be sent away for life, they wouldn't have run in the first place. When they confess, its usually the end result of exhaustive, cooperative police efforts that have gathered very specific details of the incident. The details have been pulled together in a manner that makes sense and can be followed with a measure of ease. The physical evidence has to corroborate the details. Those details are selectively laid out in front of the suspect and they have to account for their whereabout and or part in the incident. As their statement is measured against the gathered evidence the case becomes clearer. They make mistakes. They say they were here at this time or did this at that time. The facts of the case don't change because they are facts and facts are static. Their stories change because it's a story and stories are fluid. Eventually, they are backed into a corner with no way out. Depending on the person, they may then realize the jig is up. At this point, they may confess or request a lawyer. Usually, by the time this point is reached, a confession is not needed because the suspect has recanted, corrected and basically made clear the statement they initially gave was untrue.

A confession is not the end of the conversation. Yes, evidence was gathered and the details of the incident has been pieced together by officers, detectives and crime scene techs. Remember, there are always pieces of the incident lost. Some of those pieces may have been taken with the suspect. Some of those pieces are lost forever. We need details. If the suspect confesses, we must make sure that confession is legit. It is not unheard of for someone to confess to a crime they did not commit. If they did it, then they know details—details we did not tell them. We ask them to tell us what happened and to give us those missing pieces. The why is important but takes a backseat to the details of the how.

"Why? Why did you shoot this man?" It was at this moment I could see the weight of the day start to come out through her facial expressions. Tears swelled in her eyes almost immediately. They were real tears as anyone could see. She paused for a long while, quietly. Her eyes moved everywhere around the room but avoided mine. She tried to speak multiple times but the words were overtaken by whimpers. I fought the urge to say anything while she sat there in silence. Eventually, she was able to compose herself. Once composed, she said, "He raped me."

I am not a psychiatrist. I have a great deal of experience interviewing people. There is no way, no matter what any guru tells you, to consistently tell if anyone is lying. With effort and time, you can tell if your spouse is lying because you've been with them through so much. Still, any husband or wife can tell you it's hit or miss. Your children, nieces or nephews, perhaps your brother, can be deciphered over time to some consistency. Random strangers, however, are different. Some people tell lies while looking away from you. Some people tell lies while looking you directly in the eye. Some people tell lies so often and so well they even believe these lies to be true. Those lies could be undetectable. There are signs that give clues when someone is being untruthful. Those signs are not infallible. They are often vague and inconsistent, person to person, and even moment to moment. In this case, I didn't see any signs.

It is not beneath most people to attempt to justify the reason they did an unspeakable act. It is often necessary for a person to justify an act that goes against their nature. Make no mistake, murder is against the nature of man. Cognitive dissonance: the state of having inconsistent thoughts, beliefs or attitudes, especially as relating to behavioral decisions and attitude change.

Rape is a crime. It is an unforgivable act that changes the victim to their core. I can't speak from a victim's point of view but I am a father, a big brother and a son. I would do anything to spare those closest to me this pain. Rape is not justification for murder; it is a motivator. I asked the female when this had happened and had she reported the incident. She advised a week or so prior she'd "tried to" report it.

I am not a sex crime detective. I am not trained or experienced enough to gather the details of a rape from a rape victim. Furthermore, this was not a rape investigation. This was a murder investigation and I had gone off-topic.

I did what I could to bring the female back to the case at hand. I gathered the details of the case meticulously. I got the location of the weapon. I worked out the timeline. I verified that all the statements of the witnesses matched the statements of the female. I did my job. I interviewed a suspect in reference to a murder.

The victim was booked into Parish Prison.

Later in follow-up, I searched the police database and found a report in the system in reference to a possible rape. The report had been filed approximately a week and a half prior to this date. The victim was an unknown female who had come to the district to report that she had been raped. She spoke to the officer who was working the desk. As the officer interviewed her, she had become irate and left the district upset. The report advised the officer was not able to gather the details of the incident or the identity of the victim. The report stated the victim appeared intoxicated, belligerent and was reluctant to answer questions. She left before completing the report. Usually, if a victim doesn't complete the interview for a report, the report would not be written. Realizing the serious nature of the incident, the officer documented what happened just in case. There would have been no follow-up investigation because if you have no victim, you have no crime.

I contacted the officer and spoke to him in reference to this case. He advised due to the victim's failure to cooperate, there was no rape kit done. The suspect was now dead. There was no way to question him about the incident. The officer verified the victim was the same female who'd been charged with murder.

The female advised at the time of the shooting she had approached the male and asked him if he thought he was going to get away with what he'd done. The female advised that he laughed and mocked her as they stood out in the street. She told him she was going to kill him. The female said the male turned to walk away and she stepped to him and fired one shot. This action was worth a twenty-five-year sentence. The female will be fifty-five years old when she is free once again.

There is no real resolution to this case. There is no satisfaction of bringing the bad guy to justice. There is only an empathetic emptiness that is filled with an unidentifiable feeling that is a cross between guilt, sympathy, pity and anger. Who was, in fact, the bad guy in this scenario? Was it the dead man/rapist? Was it the female shooter/rape victim? Was it the police who failed to solve the rape but succeeded in solving the murder? This kind of thing doesn't wake me up in the middle of the night but if it crosses my mind, I know there will be no rest that night.

30

The Circle of Life

As an officer, my job is to maintain order in my jurisdiction. A byproduct of that job is sending a lot of people to prison. I don't know how many people I've arrested. Honestly, I don't think about the people once they're in prison. I concentrate on the people who are left behind. The victims of the crimes committed by people deserve more of my empathy.

Occasionally, I run into someone who I've put away. When this happens, first, I recall who they are. Then, I think about how long they were gone and what kind of damage that time away has done to the family. I know prison is supposed to be a place where people are rehabilitated and returned back to society. It's supposed to be, but I'm not a simpleton. I know criminals often come out worse than when they went in. I know the government has cut all the funds and programs to prisons. They have changed the prison system from a place of rehabilitation to a place where little criminals get their stripes and level up. For this, I'm sorry. The last thing I ever want to do is add to the problem. That being said, the system in place is the system we have. It's the only system I have to work with. If the only other option is to keep the wolves among the sheep, then it is better the wolves be kept with wolves.

The call was an elderly man who had been beaten to death. The scene was the local old folks' hangout, a double driveway with a covered awning, a few tables set up where the old men in the neighborhood who drank too much played spades and dominoes. I'd passed by this spot many times. Every time I had, there were people there and music playing. Not that day. That day, there was just one person there. He was an elderly man, sixtyish, sitting on the ground. He was sitting up with his back against a bench. His clothing was ruffled and he had a small cut at the corner of his mouth. There was a broken gin bottle and a chair knocked over but nothing else was really out of place.

Speaking to the crowd standing behind the signature yellow tape, I eventually got told about a young man and a fight. Witnesses advised a younger, fitter man had walked up to the hangout spot. The "young man" was described as between thirty-five and forty years old. He was described as muscular and in shape. He had begun to curse and argue with the old man. The young man accused the old man of "talking" to his girl. There was something about an incident at a club. The old man told the young man, he didn't want any problems. The young man was irate. The old man told him, "Leave me the fuck alone. I don't play with you young dudes." The young man approached the old man and punched him in the face. The old man was heavily out-matched. The young man punched the old man multiple times. The old man fell to the ground against a bench and didn't get up. The young man boasted for a moment before leaving the area on foot.

It wasn't long before we had a positive identification of the suspect. Oddly enough, the man hadn't had any reports in our system. For someone to have perpetrated an act of such violence, we expected a slew of police reports going back years. Such is usually the case. Not a single report was found going back ten years. The suspect was picked up not far from the scene and was transported to my office. Another detective and I sat down with the young man. He was read his rights per Miranda and signed the waiver. The other detective and I sat down prepared for a long, drawn out interview. We knew this was going to be like pulling teeth to get the information we needed. I was mistaken. The second detective began to laugh and talk with the young man. The topic apparently didn't matter. We talked about neighborhoods and the past few years. The young man had missed a lot. He'd only been free for about a year. It turns out the young man had been in prison for the last twenty years for "manslaughter." He was forty years old and had been in prison since he was nineteen. By the time we got to the conversation about the old man, we were good friends. We'd bonded on a personal level. With our new dynamic in place, we asked the young man what happened with the old man.

The young man described the chain of events in good detail. A couple days prior, he and his girlfriend had been in a local hole in the wall night club. While there, he talked with people, including a few females. His girlfriend, who did not appreciate his friendliness toward the females, spent her time sitting at the bar. While she was there, the old man bought her a drink. She accepted the drink and she and the old man talked. When the young man noticed, he was upset. The young man approached the old man and "checked" him. The young man let the old man know, in no uncertain terms, that this was his girl. "She don't need no sugadaddy." The young man said the old man tried to talk sporty, like he wasn't afraid. The bouncers saw the disturbance and decided to put the young man out. The young man told the old man he would wait outside and they could settle this like men. The old man declined the invitation. The young man waited outside but the old man never came out. The old man slipped out the back of the club to avoid the conflict.

A few days later, the young man saw the old man at the old folks' hangout spot. He approached the old man and asked him,

"What's up now?" The old man was again talking "sporty" and so the young man had to "deal" with him. "Deal with him?" the second detective asked. The old man then said "Yeah, I had to whup him." The second detective said, "You beat him?"

"Hell yeah."

I asked, "Did the old-timer get any licks in?"

"Shid, he ain't have a chance."

It was at this point the young man stood up in the interview room. He began to shadow box in a demonstration of how he engaged a sixty-year-old man in a fistfight—a fistfight resulting in his death. The second detective and I responded appropriately to keep the current ambiance going. We kept the pretense that we were just guys talking. I asked, "Did you drop him?"

"Did I!"

The young man was still enthusiastic about the fight. After we were sure we made our case, we asked the question we both knew would sober the mood of the moment.

"Was he still alive when you left?"

"Alive! Yeah, he was alive!"

Apparently, the young man didn't realize the old man was dead. The young man was booked into prison. He was charged, for the second time in his life, with manslaughter. He was, for the second time in his life, sentenced to twenty years in prison. When he is released, he will be the old man.

31

The Last Chapter

I am a black officer. I would be remiss if I were to ignore the current state of affairs. I have to look at this from more than one point of view. I have to look at it as a minority who grew up in an area where the minority was underrepresented in the local police department. I also have to look at it from a seasoned officer's point of view. From my years of being an officer, I know that often, the officer is just as afraid as the civilian. He doesn't know what he is going to encounter and is on edge starting out. However, I'm no fool. I know there are those officers who misuse their power to assert an authority they don't actually have.

I am thirty-nine years old and have been a police officer for over fifteen years. My hands still shake when I get pulled over by the police. I have had numerous experiences that I would consider bad with the police.

Just recently, I was with my wife and son in a very non-threatening vehicle (green Honda Element). We were on a long drive, and my son was in his car seat. I noticed my son's seat was propped up, and he could not sleep comfortably. I then pulled over to the side of the road. I adjusted my kid's seat and got back into the driver seat. I buckled my seatbelt and started to negotiate back into traffic. It was at this moment a state trooper's unit pulled up behind me with his lights activated. The trooper did not exit his vehicle; he just parked behind me with his lights going. I stayed in the car and waited for orders. Approximately three minutes passed, and the trooper said nothing. I released my foot from the gas and allowed the vehicle to move forward. The trooper hit his siren to give me the order to stop. I opened the car door to step out, and he yelled through the loudspeaker, "Get back in the car!" I did as he ordered. I assumed he would tell me why he was there eventually. After another five minutes, he had said nothing else to me. I waited another seven minutes. Eventually, the officer approached the vehicle and told me to step to the rear of the vehicle. He was hostile. I gave him my license, registration and insurance. He was standing chest to chest with me yelling, "Why were you try to leave?"

"Because you didn't stop me. I was already—"

Before I could finish my sentence, he yelled, "Why'd you keep trying to get out of the car?" The trooper appeared to be truly upset. I stopped talking. The whole time I was in contact with this trooper, I was concerned about my family in the car. I eventually told this trooper that I was a police officer. It was at this point his whole demeanor changed. He responded, "Where is your commission." I slowly reached into my back pocket to get it. After he inspected the commission, he spoke to me with respect. He almost immediately cut me loose.

He had no reason to come into contact with me. He did not stop me, as I was already on the side of the road. If anything, he should have asked me if I needed assistance. Instead, he treated me as a suspect with no charge. He detained me while he searched the police database for my license plate. When he found nothing, he approached me with open hostility. He presumed to assert an authority that he did not have. Perhaps this was an isolated incident.

Here is another example, just one more of many. I was on

my motorcycle on a beautiful Sunday afternoon. I was exiting my rocky driveway, which is in a very rural area. I waited for some cars to pass before pulling out of my driveway. As I pulled out into the road, some of the rocks gave way under my wheels. This caused me to pull out slower than I intended. As a result, a car had to slow down, a gold-colored Grand Am. Mind you, the car didn't have to slow down to avoid hitting me. Nope. I just slowed its pace before I picked up speed and continued on my way. As I said, it was Sunday, and I was out for a joyride. I did not speed. I did not swerve past the yellow dotted line. I first rode out of my town into the next, which was a small town. The speed limit was forty-five mph. Like many small towns, this one received a large portion of its annual budget from traffic tickets. As I have been stopped many times, I never speed through this town. I usually put my vehicle on cruise control to make sure I don't speed. This time, I was on the bike, so I was even more cautious. The town was so small that even at forty-five miles per hour, I was completely through town two in about five minutes. I made it through without incident. The gold-colored Grand Am was still right behind me. As I entered town three, which was actually a decent size town, I continued at the same speed. This town could be traversed in about twenty minutes at a forty-five mph pace.

About midway through this town, I saw blue lights in my rearview. I pulled over at a grocery store only to find that the officer who pulled me over was an officer from town two. I pulled over and took off my helmet. The officer asked me for my driver's license, which I provided. At the same time, I noticed the gold-colored Grand Am has pulled up behind the officer, which anyone can tell you is a no-no. The driver of the gold-colored Grand Am was a tall, bearded, white man in camouflage-colored pants and a sleeveless camouflage shirt. He walked around the officer as if he was not there. The officer called in my license and completely ignored the man as he approached me. Tall Man asked me if I knew who he was. I remained silent because I was flustered and disturbed by the chain of events unfolding.

When I am pulled over, I am always nervous. I have no idea if I am going to be dealing with some prick. My hands shake, and the best way I can describe it is I feel as if I am naked. While I was feeling exposed, this tall camouflaged man walked up to me.

Tall Man told me he as the Sheriff of Norwood, Louisiana. That meant absolutely nothing to me. I didn't even know where Norwood, Louisiana was. I did know it was nowhere near there. Tall Man told me I cut him off when I pulled out of my driveway.

As I mentally put together what had happened, I became enraged. An officer from town two stopped me in town three. The officer from town two had no jurisdiction in town three; yet, he stopped me anyway. He stopped me at the behest of a sheriff who had no jurisdiction in any of the three towns. The sheriff clearly called the local police chief of town two and told him to get one of his guys to stop me. This was a clear abuse of power.

Here I am, standing in a parking lot naked with two dudes who are exercising power they don't have. When you strip away the legal authority of a police officer, you are left with a prepared man with a weapon. That is still a very dangerous scenario for anyone who has anything to live for.

Please notice I never said these officers stopped me because I'm black. There is no way for me to say that was the case. I know the trooper saw me get back into my vehicle. I know the sheriff saw me on my bike. I will say that I have been stopped and mistreated more than my fair share. I can say that when I speak with my friends of color, these stories seem commonplace. I can also say when I speak with my other friends, they do not report similar experiences. That may be a coincidence, or it may be the standard.

Only someone who can walk both sides of the street can say for sure.

If I had to give advice to the minority population, which I do feel obligated to do, I would say, humble yourself. You should not have to any more than anyone else in the world. It is not fair. It is not right. However, it is necessary. It will be hard. I know from personal experience that swallowing pride is difficult. I also know that sons need their fathers as much as daughters do. Understand that I do want you to fight. I just want you to fight to win.

Before anyone loses his or her mind, bear with me for a moment. I've seen people arguing with officers out on the street. You will not win an argument with an officer. If the situation escalates, you will not win. I recommend you lose the battle out there on the street. You were likely to lose it anyway. If the officer speaks to you in an inappropriate manner, go with it. If he violates your rights, mention it but go with it. If you are lucky enough to be released after the incident, then go straight to internal affairs and follow up. There are cameras. Everyone has a phone. Officers tend to be on their best behavior because they don't know who is recording. If you file a complaint saying something illegal, immoral or just wrong has occurred, the department will investigate. With all of the cameras both on the department and civilian population, no one knows what was captured. When the officer is questioned about the situation, he will have to respond. If he is an idiot, he will lie. That is a very dangerous proposition. If there is footage that contradicts his statement, his integrity is now in question. That is a dangerous predicament for an officer. If he lies about one thing, it's assumed he lies about others. He will likely be suspended, and other complaints about him will be reexamined. This is the case if he just spoke in a disrespectful manner. If he broke the law, he will likely be fired and may face criminal charges. Religion aside, being in prison will be hell for a police officer.

On the opposite side of the fence, there are people who lie. Someone will file a complaint on an officer, and it will be a complete falsehood. Every part of the story is a lie, and there is usually video to prove it. I think the problem the department makes is they don't charge these folks with filing a false police report. The officer should be able to sue the person. The integrity of any person, especially an officer, is a precious thing. It should not be called into question unjustly. If it is called into question and found to be sound, reparations should be made. The same applies to civilians. They sue officers to get their reparations. I think the same avenue should be available to the police. Of course, it is not, because of the nature of the job.

I am not perfect. I make mistakes. I am a law enforcement officer. It does not pay well and the hours are not great. I have other talents but this is my calling. I don't want to discourage anyone from taking this path. I do want you to take careful consideration before you do. This path is not for the faint of heart. The rewards are few. After thirty years of sixty-hour workweeks, you will likely be forgotten by those who depended on you to risk everything so they may have peace. That is the way of things and we have all chosen our own paths.

In closing. I hope we now have a better understanding of police officers and what they do. Police officers want to make sure the job is done and everyone goes home safe. That includes the officer. The next time you see a police officer, feel free to see if he has a moment. Ask a few questions and get to know the people tasked with protecting you and the rest of the people of this nation. I am Webalization, and I approved this message.

Made in the USA
Las Vegas, NV
18 November 2020